Battleground Europe

SOMME

Serre

This guide is dedicated to the memory of all those men from every corner of the British Isles, her Empire and from France who took part in the preparations for, or who were there on, the days of the four battles to wrest the hamlet of Serre from the German Army. In particular it is dedicated to my uncle, George Halton, of the Burnley Company, 11th (S) Battalion (Accrington Pals) The East Lancashire Regiment, who, though badly wounded and after lying out in No Man's Land for four days, survived to tell the story in later years to me, his nephew. Also it is dedicated to his brother-in-law, my father, who fought over the same ground two years later with the Royal Field Artillery, attached to the 42nd (East Lancashire) Division.

Jack Horsfall

To this I would add a dedication to the present inhabitants of the towns and villages on the old battlefields of the Somme who show so much tolerance to the many thousands of pilgrims who come back every year and walk their fields.

Nigel Cave

Other guides in the Battleground Europe Series:

THE SOMME: BEAUMONT HAMEL

THE SOMME: THIEPVAL

YPRES: SANCTUARY WOOD & HOOGE

ARRAS: VIMY RIDGE

Cover painting: **'Zero Hour' by James Prinsep Beadle, by courtesy of the Trustees of the Imperial War Museum.**

Overleaf: **The village of Serre, finally in British hands after the German withdrawal to the Hindenberg Line in 1917.**

Battleground Europe

SOMME

Serre

Jack Horsfall
and
Nigel Cave

LEO COOPER
London

First published in 1996 by
LEO COOPER
190 Shaftesbury Avenue, London WC2H 8JL
an imprint of
Pen & Sword Books Limited
47 Church Street, Barnsley, South Yorkshire S70 2AS

ISBN 0 85052 508 X

A CIP catalogue of this book is available
from the British Library

Printed by Redwood Books Limited
Trowbridge, Wiltshire

*For up-to-date information on other titles produced under the Leo
Cooper imprint, please telephone or write to:*

Pen & Sword Books Ltd, FREEPOST, 47 Church Street
Barnsley, South Yorkshire S70 2AS
Telephone 01226 734555

CONTENTS

ACKNOWLEDGEMENTS

The help of Regimental Secretaries and curators of military museums has been invaluable; the list of these would be too great to place here. All regimental museums of the battalions that fought at Serre, were most willing to assist. Regimental histories, War Diary extracts and other valuable material was often forthcoming. Assistance from Souvenir Français, especially from its very active Arras branch, was very much appreciated, as were a number of German contacts.

Mr David Leighton has kindly allowed us to publish material relating to Roland Leighton. Colonel Pat Love of the Worcesters' Regimental Museum has helped tremendously with this aspect of the book.

I am grateful to the Taylor Library and to Mr Terry Carter for allowing us to use a number of their photographs. The cover painting is from the Imperial War Museum and we acknowledge their permission to reproduce it.

I am most grateful to Richard Brucciani who flew me over France in his light aircraft and then performed artistic pirouettes in the sky at my behest as I searched for some feature or other on the ground. It is a tremendous experience to see the Somme battlefield from the air. I am indebted to Paul Fisher for driving Jack Horsfall and myself to the Somme and then accompanying us on our somewhat chilly walks around the battlefield at Serre. I am also grateful to him for taking the time to look over some of the text. Mark Fisher accompanied me on a weekend trip to France to finalise photographs and routes; he also read through the proofs. Once more my father, Colonel Terry Cave, has read through parts of the book and I am appreciative for his advice and assistance.

The Commonwealth War Graves Commission has been most helpful. It lent me numerous cemetery registers at a very modest charge, and I would recommend this to those who remove registers from cemeteries in France and Belgium. The irritation and disappointment that this causes is great, and one can only hope that this dreadful interference with the cemeteries will cease.

The growing numbers of Britons living on the Somme provided a cheery welcome at various parts of the day, especially when the weather was ghastly. Thanks for hospitality are due to Janet and Tom Fairgrieve at Delville Wood, to Avril Williams at Auchonvillers and to Mike and Julie Renshaw at Beaumont Hamel.

We are both very appreciative of the friendly and understanding manner of the French inhabitants of Hebuterne and Serre. I am sure that they think that we are all slightly mad, but they tolerate us walking over fields, avoid our cars on tiny roads and tracks by driving over fields and generally adopt a cheery attitude. I am not sure that their British equivalents would be quite so benevolent.

My fellow author is Jack Horsfall. To me has fallen the task of working with him on the script and producing the finished article. Jack has been going to Serre for many years now and has a real feel for a particularly special place for him. I hope that I have done justice to him in my work on the book.

A view looking north over the left hand flank of the Somme battlefield.

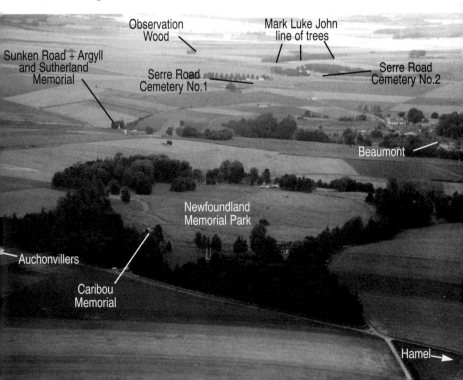

INTRODUCTION AND ADVICE TO TRAVELLERS

Serre is a tiny place, a one street hamlet on a wind-swept ridge on the Somme. It is a village whose name meant a lot to towns and cities in Britain's industrial north such as Sheffield, Leeds, Bradford, Durham, Barnsley and Hull. In recent years it has once more appeared in the limelight, mainly due to a series of books about the Pals battalions, many of which were in the 31st Division that fought at that terrible place on 1st July 1916.

This book is about Serre, but the fact should never be forgotten that it was but one piece in the large jigsaw that formed the battle line on that fateful day. In addition it was famous for only two days (13th November being the other) in the whole of that four and a half month battle. Sight should not be lost of the whole picture, which in the case of the Somme was of a great grinding down battle, which also provided the armies of Britain and her Empire with a training ground in blood and death.

Serre is at the northern end of the Somme battlefield. Accommodation in Arras might be considered a possibility and there are numerous hotels, including chains such as Ibis and the cheap but reliable Hotel Formule 1. In Albert there are several hotels; I have traditionally stayed at the de la Paix which is near the centre of town on the road out to Amiens; the Basilique is in the square opposite the basilica, and there are others.

There are a number of hotels in Bapaume and Péronne and accommodation is generally not a problem except in the period around 1st July.

Bed and Breakfasts are a recent phenomenon. There are two in Auchonvillers - Avril Williams in the village, Tel 22 76 23 66 and Mike and Julie Renshaw at Les Galets, their house just behind the old British front line before Hawthorn Crater, Tel 22 76 28 79. There is one French-run establishment in Mailly-Maillet which has been recommended to me. At Courcelette Paul Reed has recently opened one, 'Sommecourt', and he also offers his services as a battlefield guide.

Maps are essential for a battlefield tour. The Commonwealth War Graves Commission produces the standard Michelin map overprinted with details of its cemeteries and memorials. It, and details about the graves and commemorations of the dead of Britain and her Empire, may be obtained from their UK headquarters: 2, Marlow Road,

Newfoundland Memorial Park

Hawthorn Crater

Beaumont

Memorial Chapel

Serre Road Cemetery No.2

Serre Road Cemetery No.1

French Military Cemetery

Serre Road Cemetery No.3

Maidenhead, Berks SL6 7DX. When asking about casualties you must be as specific as possible, as there were some million or so British dead in the Great War. You should get the Green series 1:100000 IGN (the French equivalent of the Ordnance Survey) No 4 for navigation and the Blue series (1:25000) Bapaume West and possibly Bapaume East if you wish to do more detailed work.

The battlefields are still potentially dangerous places, and you should treat all projectiles and old munitions with great respect. These things still kill people every year. Please always remember the basic courtesies when walking on other people's land and respect the farmers' livelihood, their crops.

Bring with you a pair of good walking boots, especially if the weather has been poor. Some of the walks go over potentially very muddy ground. Some sort of waterproof would be a good idea, whatever the season. A camera (and tripod for photographs of individual graves) is essential, as well as plenty of film,

9

preferably bought in the UK as it is much cheaper there. You should take a notebook of some sort to record the details of the photographs taken, as your memory may well go blank when confronted with photographs of fields. Always try and ensure that you have a recognisable feature, and with old trenches and shell holes try and get someone or an object in them so that you are given a sense of scale and depth. A corkscrew is invaluable for the picnic, along with a sharp knife to deal with the essential baguette. A pair of binoculars is always useful.

There are relatively few cafes in this area. Avril Williams in Auchonvillers sells hot and cold drinks, including beer; there is a new cafe by Beaucourt station and a very pleasant restaurant and bar at Authuille. Bucquoy has a supermarket, petrol station and one or two bars. Further south the South African Memorial at Delville Wood has a museum, a cafe (non-alcoholic hot and cold drinks only), a very interesting and extensive bookshop, good clean toilets and a picnic area.

There are two museums within easy access. The museum in the old air raid shelters by the basilica in Albert is open for most of the year except the winter months and has some fascinating exhibits.

At the southern end of the Somme battlefield, the *Historial* at Péronne has a tremendous exhibition, videos and films. It is an ideal place to go when the weather makes battlefield visiting a chore rather than a pleasure.

We would advise comprehensive insurance cover for yourself and the car. Bring all the medication that you are likely to need and ensure that your tetanus jab is up to date. These precautions may sound as though you are going on a campaign yourself; but a visit to the battlefield is an enjoyable, often emotional, experience.

We hope that this book helps to enhance that experience.

Right: Lieutenant-General Sir Aylmer Hunter-Weston, commander of VIII Corps for the Somme Battle (holding map), with his staff.

MAPS

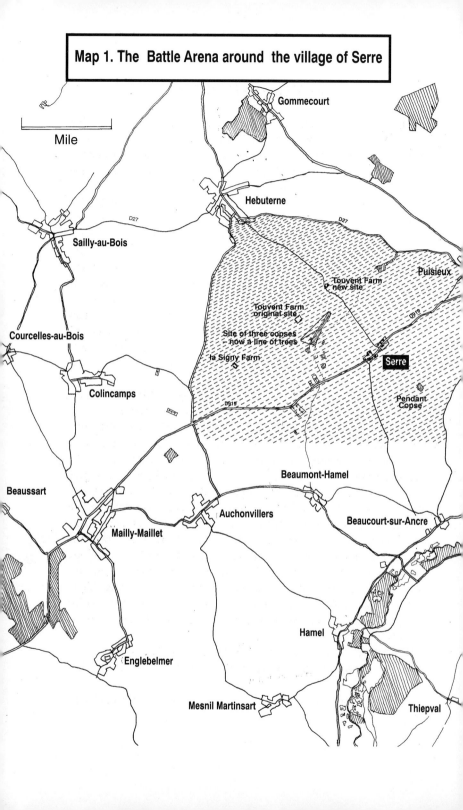

Map 1. The Battle Arena around the village of Serre

Chapter One

SETTING THE SCENE

Of all the British battlefields of the Somme many would argue that none is more emotive than the small battleground on the western side of this little village. It is made more so by the valiant and terribly costly efforts of the French army almost exactly twelve months before the great British onslaught of July 1st 1916.

This French attack provided the new line to which the British arrived late July 1915. After its capture by the Germans from the French in 1914 until the heady days for the armies of the British Empire in August 1918 Serre was never taken in battle. In February 1917 the Germans had surrendered the shattered remnants of the hamlet, but without a fight; they simply stole away in the night as a part of their general withdrawal to the Hindenburg Line, some fifteen miles to the east of Bapaume. They were back, however, when the German armies swept forward in their Ludendorff offensive in March and April 1918. Not only did they capture the village, but gained a further two thousand yards of flat land on its western side before the attack ran out of steam on this part of the line.

The Battle of the Somme commenced on July 1st 1916; the British attacked on a line of about fifteen miles from north to south.

Roughly half way down this line is Albert, which sits on the River Ancre, the town's former name. Five miles south of Albert the Front bent eastwards, forming the shape of a hockey stick at Maricourt, the end of the British attack line. At the very top of this 'hockey stick' was Serre, making it the most northern part of the entire battle (excluding the diversionary attack at Gommecourt). The strategy was that the line would swing in a great anti-clockwise arc, pivoting at Serre. This would sweep the Germans out of the valley of the Ancre, over the Pozières Ridge and onto the flat land round the town of Bapaume, eleven miles to the east. The division at Serre would swing in an anti-clockwise arc of ninety degrees so that it formed a north-facing shield, protecting the divisions south of it from German reinforcements which might be brought down into the battle from Puisieux, Bucquoy and the Achiets.

The action at Serre had a crucial part in the plans for July 1st: it was to be the essential protection for the continuing success of the 'Big Push'.

The one-street village sits on a low ridge with its twenty or so houses and farms, almost the same as it had then, spread along either side of the main road coming up from the village of Mailly-Maillet four miles south, on its way to Puisieux just a mile and a half north of Serre. Behind Serre, eastwards, the almost treeless, open, arable farming land rolls gently towards Miraumont, a large village and the source of the Ancre which flows south west and ultimately on to the Somme. This plateau, four thousand yards wide, is slashed by a deep winding valley starting below Serre and which runs down to Miraumont. Near the main road at the Serre end is a feature called Ten Tree Alley, named after the few trees at its commencement. It was a track, but in time part of it has been obliterated and returned to the plough. There is one wood which dominates the plateau, of about one acre in extent and a thousand yards or so from Serre, situated on the edge of a deep yawning hollow. This was called Pendant Copse.

Looking north-west from Serre from a high point at the south of the village the ground for five hundred yards or so is flat before it begins

The village of Serre in 1932, looking towards Serre Road No.1 Cemetery. Note the piles of war debris among which are numerous unexploded shells awaiting collection.

to drop down into a shallow valley with its cleft running parallel to the main road. In the middle distance, about a mile and a half away, you can see the spire of the church and the village of Hebuterne. Looking to your half-left you will see, a mile away, on the western edge of the valley in front of you, a group of buildings which make up La Signy Farm; following the line of that ridge northwards, just to your left, is a small copse which fills a large hole twenty yards or so in diameter – all that remains of Observation Wood. Further round still, almost directly in front of your line of sight, and on the valley's western edge, is a small stand of trees surrounding a post war small brick building, about as big as a garden shed. Here once stood Toutvent (Touvent) Farm.

The valley was of great importance for much of the fighting that took place in the area during the war. The fields stretch westwards from Serre for several hundred yards before they begin, quite gently at first, to slope downwards until after six hundred yards or so it becomes a much steeper drop. A long, fairly dense but narrow wood stretching for half a mile or so is exactly on that steep incline and in front of Serre. Behind the wood is the valley floor, flat and treeless, in places two hundred yards wide, along which once ran a narrow gauge railway

The same view in 1994

Railway Hollow Cemetery; the long line of woodland used to be three copses which were named after the evangelists Mark, Luke and John. Matthew Copse used to be over to the right in the valley and was removed to aid farming.

connecting the valley to the dump at Euston on the Colincamps road. In 1917 a British Army built broad gauge line went in front of the long wood. The western side of the valley wall is somewhat narrower, probably two hundred and fifty yards deep, going up to the La Signy Farm ridge, which is not quite as high as the one upon which Serre stands. Another tiny wood was once in the bottom of the valley, slightly south of the existing one, but after the war what was left of it was removed to give more farming land. Over the ridge, on the flat land behind Touvent Farm, there used to be yet another group of trees, Staff Copse, but that has gone also.

By 1916 the valley was named by the British, Railway Hollow. The long narrow wood used to be three small ones with twenty yards or so between each; the three copses were known (from north to south) as John, Luke and Mark, whilst the fourth wood in the valley, the most southerly, but now removed, was named Matthew. They were named after the four Evangelists. The significance of John is that much greater in that its northern extremity was itself the northern point of the great battle of July 1st, the hinge on which so much depended.

Looking south, down the main road towards Mailly, you will see on each side of it some more trees, but these are new. They commence at the start of the special track that was put in to facilitate the maintenance and visiting of the four cemeteries in the valley, where numbers of those killed here lie buried. On the opposite side of the main road from where this track starts began what was called Ten Tree

16

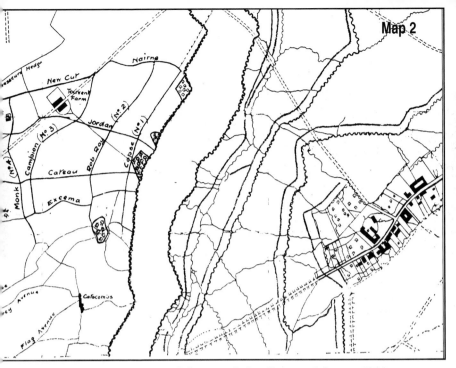

A section of a battle map of Serre and the German defences, 1916. Matthew Copse is now gone and Mark, Luke and John are joined together to make one long stretch of trees.

Alley. Behind the new trees, on the western side of the road, is a large farm house and beyond that is a large British cemetery, Serre Number 1. It was filled only after the fighting for Serre was over, when the battlefields were cleared.

Next to it is a French National Cemetery, created by the British after the war was over and handed over to the French government in 1933. On the other side of the road is a small church, erected in the 1930s to commemorate their dead. It is usually closed, but on the closest Sunday to the great battle of June 1915 a special mass is offered for those who fell. It has a porch and on its northern wall is a small tablet erected by German veterans in remembrance of their brave comrades who died at Serre.

Half a mile or so further down the road is the largest British cemetery in the Somme area, holding the remains of seven and a half thousand men. Started in 1917, it is called Serre Number 2 and has been placed on the site of a large German Redoubt, the *Heidenkopf*, known to the British as the 'Quadrilateral'. It was arrow head in shape, its deep, wide trenches and formidable barriers of barbed wire entanglements pointing menacingly at the British line on the opposite side of the road.

Within the village the small orchards have been replanted, but there remains in them, and in the ground between the houses, many indications of the German fortifications, lines of trenches and the indentations of shell craters. Some of the land seems to have been barely disturbed since the war. In 1916 the village was surrounded by a four-deep trench system which included vast dugouts some of which were thirty feet deep and well protected against the heaviest shell fire, with a multiplicity of entrances.

Deep barbed wire entanglements defended the trenches whilst the villagers' cellars were turned into an underground barracks. The Germans had worked hard since arriving at Serre in September 1914 to turn it into a fort, one of many created along the Front Line on the west.

There are only four permanent memorials to commemorate all the heroism that was performed here by the British - that is apart from the strikingly eloquent evidence of the cemeteries. One is in the village, dedicated to the members of the Sheffield City Battalion, 12th (Service) Battalion, Yorks and Lancs. Another, dedicated to the men of the 11th (Service) Battalion, East Lancs, the 'Accrington Pals', has been recently placed in Mark Copse. In between Mark and Luke Copse is a small archway put there by Yorkshiremen and dedicating the wood

Trees in front of the village of Serre with indications in the ground where German positions once were.

The only section of trenches on the Somme preserved by the British are to be found in the wood that once was known as Mark, Luke and John Copses. The edge of the trees on top of the slope indicate where the British front line once was.

as Sheffield Park. It is the only part of the front line that has been preserved by the British, a stark contrast to the Dominion memorials at Vimy, Delville Wood and Beaumont Hamel. Perhaps the most poignant of the memorials is the fourth, a large cross erected on the front line in Luke Copse, which marks the spot where Pte AE Bull of the Sheffield City Battalion was found in 1928, twelve years after he was killed on July 1st 1916, presumably at the selfsame spot. He was reinterred at Serre Road No 2 cemetery (XIX E 16). In the wood the trenches have been left much as they were, their depth and stark lines softened by time as are the great shell craters. The entrances to dugouts and saps may be discerned. Doubtless the ground still holds the remains of many men whose bodies were never recovered, some blown to small pieces, others hurriedly buried in trenches or shell holes which were later destroyed by shell fire. The whole of the valley was slashed with trenches, dug first by the Germans, then by the French and then by the British.

All the trenches were given names, with sign boards along them and direction indicators, for all the world a subterranean version of a suburban street system. In front of the wood were the British barbed wire defences, with a broad belt of No Man's Land running between them and their German equivalents. The three cemeteries in front of the woods are all in this deadly slice of land. Leading out of the valley and up the western slopes were long communication trenches so that troops could make their way in and out of the valley and up to the firing line in comparative safety.

A good place to start the pilgrimage to Serre is at Albert, the town which became a conduit to the front for the vast numbers of men from Britain and her Empire that went out to fight on the dreaded Somme front. The striking golden statue of the Madonna and Child on the top of the basilica is still the dominant sight in the town, although now standing safely upright and not at the crazy angle to which it was reduced for most of the war. Underneath the square, in front of the church, is the newly opened Albert Museum, dedicated to the 1914-1918 period. Access is from the Rue de Birmingham (the city to which Albert was twinned after 1918 as part of the post-war reconstruction) and the exhibition has improved steadily in quality since its opening a few years ago. A range of souvenirs and publications are available at the exit, in the town's park. This museum visit should help to make the visit to the battlefield that much more interesting, having seen the equipment, maps and uniforms that were used or worn by the combatants of some eighty or more years ago.

Chapter Two

THE FIRST BATTLE
7th – 13th June, 1915

By the end of 1914 the Germans had established themselves in their most westward position in the north with a front two thousand yards or so in front of Serre, knocking at the door of Hebuterne. The line bordered the north east part of the high ground on which Hebuterne stands and continued south between the ridge top farms of Toutvent and La Signy before continuing its way towards Beaumont and Albert. During the winter of 1914 and the spring of 1915 the Germans dug deeply to consolidate their position, in this sector forming a salient three thousand yards long and a thousand yards in depth, west of Touvent Farm. This farm they had turned into a formidable stronghold and from which they had a commanding view to the west across the six miles deep Hebuterne-Colincamps Plain. These two hill top villages are approximately three thousand yards apart.

The small villages on this plain were the bases and camps of the French and then the British armies, even though they were within long distance shelling range and so much under the eyes of the Germans. Consequently Sailly-au-Bois, Courcelles, Couin, Bus-les-Artois, Bertrancourt, Authie and others were hardly safe places to be. Nevertheless they had to be used to sustain the troops at the front in the Serre sector.

In the planning for 1915 the French army had two objectives for the Hebuterne sector. The first was to eliminate the Touvent Farm salient and capture the ridge top hamlet of Serre, thereby giving them a commanding view of the Ancre Valley and threatening the German positions to the south. The second was to create a diversion from the sector to the north around Arras, where the French had launched a major offensive against the Lorette Spur and Vimy Ridge in May. Such an attack, it was hoped, would force the Germans to withdraw some of their forces to the north of Arras, or at the very least make them keep their troops, including reserves, in the Hebuterne sector.

The French troops in this sector were part of the Second Army under the command of General Noel Marie de Castelnau. He was an aristocrat and a devout Catholic; he was a lay member of a religious order and consequently known as *'Le Capuchin Botté'* (the booted friar).When Joffre was appointed French Commander in Chief in 1912

General Noel Marie de Castelnau commander of the Second Army. A firm believer in the policy of attack, he directed French operations to take the village of Serre in the summer of 1915.

he became his chief of staff and was a key contributor to the ill-fated Plan XVII, the French plan of action on the outbreak of hostilities. He had fought in the Franco-Prussian War of 1870-1871 and reacted to the defensive strategy which had characterised the French effort in that conflict. He firmly believed in attack and attack again with the utmost speed and tenacity, and could not easily countenance the thought that part of sacred France should be occupied by the invader.

One of the consequences of his mentality – widespread at the time in the French army – was that they concentrated their resources on a quick-firing, light field gun which should be highly mobile to support the infantry's dashing attacks. This requirement resulted in the famous French '75', an excellent weapon and the best of its class amongst any of the combatants. It had a useful service life in the Second World War. The Germans, on the other hand, had developed a family of artillery pieces and thus had a great advantage well into the conflict in the sort of warfare into which the Western Front degenerated.

The famous French '75' was developed as a supporting light artillery piece for the attacking infantry and proved to be a successful weapon throughout the war.

Like most French commanders de Castelnau could not tolerate the thought of the German invader on French soil and vigorously pursued an all out offensive policy.

The battle was scheduled to commence on 7th June, 1915. After what was thought to be a damaging bombardment of the German lines, de Castelnau launched three regiments of infantry, the 65th, 93rd and 137th, on a front of two thousand yards against the German line. Their start point was from positions close to the Colincamps-Hebuterne road, near to the Quarries. The attack started at 8 am and had a time scale of ten minutes to capture two lengths of German trenches and Toutvent Farm. The farm did not fall in this seemingly impossible short time, but parts of their first two lines did. The enemy counter- attacked strongly twice during the remainder of the day, but on both occasions were beaten off and failed to retake the trenches they had lost to the three French regiments.

The French losses on that first day, attacking over open ground, were 1,400 killed, wounded and missing – roughly one man for each yard of trench that had been captured. The new position that they occupied was exposed, however, and the situation could not be allowed to rest there.

The attack was resumed at 3 am on 8th June, on a new objective a thousand yards to the north around La Louvière Farm, this time by the 75th and 14th Regiments. The Germans vigorously repelled the assault, inflicting heavy losses on both regiments; but they too had suffered, and now realised that the French were not simply making a diversionary attack. It was now obvious that the French were making a full-blooded attempt to take Serre.

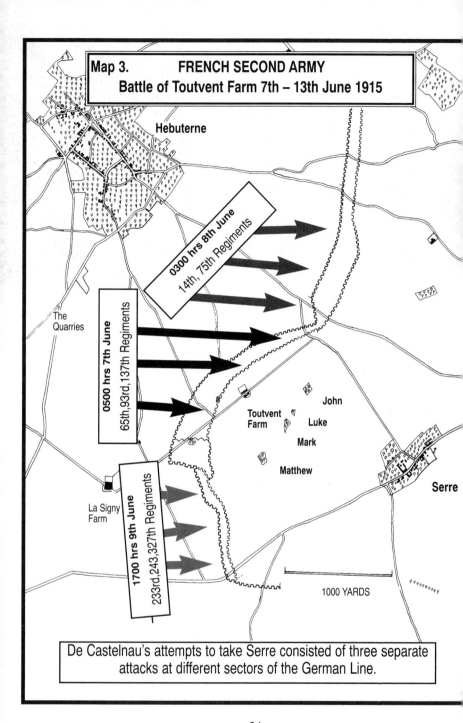

Map 3.   FRENCH SECOND ARMY
Battle of Toutvent Farm 7th – 13th June 1915

Hebuterne

0300 hrs 8th June
14th, 75th Regiments

The Quarries

0500 hrs 7th June
65th,93rd,137th Regiments

John

Toutvent Farm   Luke

Mark

Matthew

Serre

La Signy Farm

1700 hrs 9th June
233rd,243,327th Regiments

1000 YARDS

De Castelnau's attempts to take Serre consisted of three separate attacks at different sectors of the German Line.

French troops occupying a German trench after a successful attack await a counter attack – usually preceeded by an artillery barrage. Rifles and equipment litter the scene.

The hot summer weather was exhausting and all those involved suffered badly from thirst. Relief came on the afternoon of 8th June when a violent storm broke over the battlefield. Whilst the thirst of the combatants was now alleviated, the ground was turned into a sticky quagmire.

De Castelnau determined on continuing the attack, sticking to his military principle of the supremacy of the attack. He changed the focus of the next onslaught to the south, as far as the road from Serre to Mailly-Maillet, at a point where the track from La Signy Farm joins the road just before it goes up the slight incline to the cross roads at the sugar factory. Three fresh regiments were to be used, the 243rd and 347th at the front of the assault with the 233rd in reserve.

The attack was hindered by the weather. Persistent fog caused a delay in the initial artillery bombardment and thus it was not until 5 pm on the evening of 9th June that the new attack got under way. As was so often the case the bombardment was insufficient to deal with the thickly laid barricade of barbed wire and the initial assault was broken up by it. However, the French persisted with a reckless bravery that characterised much of their fighting in 1914 and 1915. They pushed the Germans back to their second line positions.

The French assault continued over the next two days, 10th and 11th June, whilst the ground gained was consolidated despite a ferocious German artillery bombardment to hamper them. The three attacking regiments were relieved by new troops. These had to face a massive German attack on the night of the 12th, but the new line held despite the vigour of the German assault.

De Castelnau was not content with his gains and resumed his attack against Toutvent Farm and Serre on 13th June using the 327th and the survivors of the 233rd and 243rd Regiments. They drove the enemy from their Second Line and actually had some prospect of being able to capture the great prize, Serre itself. However, the Second Army's casualties had been so enormous, and its units so damaged, that a further attempt on the tiny village could not be made.

The battle of 7th – 13th June had cost the French dearly. Approximately 2,000 officers and men were killed, with nearly 9,000 wounded and missing – making a total of around 11,000 casualties on a front only two miles long and a thousand yards deep. It was a heavy sacrifice with a great prize so near the taking. The consequences for the Germans of losing the ridge upon which Serre sits would have been considerable, threatening their position to the south; it is unlikely that they would have acquiesced to such a situation and would have done their utmost to remove the French.

Nevertheless, much of the salient had been reduced and now the French Front Line in front of Serre was 500 yards east of Toutvent

After the battle. By the time the French offensive came to an end some 2,000 French soldiers were dead and almost 9,000 were either wounded or missing.

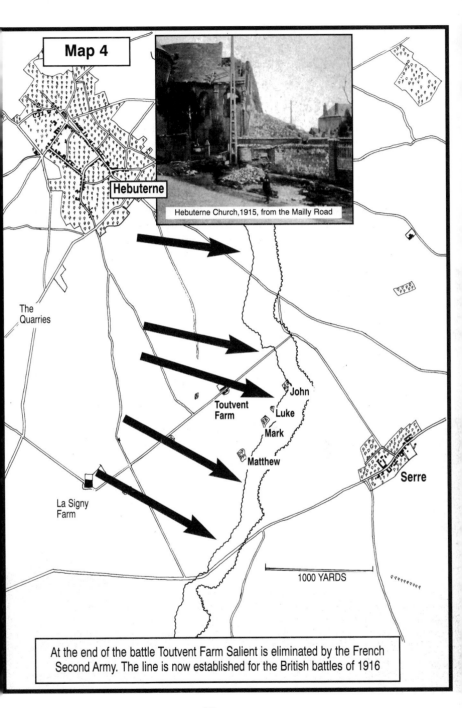

Map 4

Hebuterne

Hebuterne Church,1915, from the Mailly Road

The Quarries

Toutvent Farm

John
Luke
Mark

Matthew

Serre

La Signy Farm

1000 YARDS

At the end of the battle Toutvent Farm Salient is eliminated by the French Second Army. The line is now established for the British battles of 1916

French troops occupying trenches in front of the Serre positions. Little attempt was made to smarten up the trench system – after all, they had no intention of staying long.

Farm, on the eastern side of Railway Hollow. The Germans' new line ran in parallel to it at an average distance of 300 yards, producing the No Man's Land that the British would soon inherit. In that extraordinary change that was so common in this war, this violent and

After the attacks of June a live and let live attitude took hold in the French sector.

A Regimental Colonel decorates one of his men with the Croix de Guerre for gallantry against the enemy.

sanguinary sector reverted almost immediately to the 'live and let live' routine that was characteristic of much of the French line.

What had been achieved? It had forced the Germans to redeploy some troops, and the Lorette Spur was captured in the north, although it might be difficult to prove a causal relationship. The position at Serre was a rather more comfortable one for the French than hitherto, and the Germans had lost something of a buffer between the front and the vital position of Serre itself. Other than that, it was a rather expensive 'small' offensive, one that was all too common a feature of the allied efforts in 1915.

Not that this effected de Castlenau much. Indeed, perhaps one of the reasons for the closing down of the offensive at Serre was his own removal from command of the Second Army on 13th June. This was not to be for a period of military re-education, or even to be Limoged, ie removed from active command, but rather to be Commander of the Central Group of Armies. His position in the Second Army was to be taken over by one of France's most controversial military figures, Henri Pétain.

As commander of his Army Group, de Castelnau was in charge of the costly and rather ineffectual Champagne Campaign that commenced in September. By this stage in the war the French had suffered getting on for 2,000,000 casualties. There had to be a change in military doctrine. He was relegated from his active command and remained out of favour in 1916 and 1917, but he bounced back to take part as a commander of armies once more in the last months of the war.

On 7th July representative units of the Second Army were visited by President Poincaré and their military supremo, General Joffre. They had arrived by car in Hebuterne and inspected elements of the regiments before leaving at about 6 pm.

It was a fitting visit as this was to be the last battle that the French fought at Serre; towards the end of July the sector was handed over to the British and Pétain's new command moved further south. The British set about improving their trenches, giving a decent burial to as many of the hundreds of corpses littering the battlefields as they could and learning the routine of trench warfare. Many of the trenches retained their French names, at least for a while; by some cartographical error never corrected, Toutvent Farm lost its second 't' on British trench maps.

This now rather sleepy sector was to be the scene of one of the best known of all the innumerable romantic tragedies of the Great War.

General Joffre visiting his units in the field.

Chapter Three

THE GERMAN DEFENDERS OF SERRE, 1914-1916

The German 52nd Division had arrived here early in 1915 and occupied the land between the two hilltop villages of Serre and Hebuterne, establishing its front line some two thousand yards west of Serre, running due north for five thousand yards towards Gommecourt, starting its southern flank two hundred yards below the Heidenkopf, their redoubt which in 1916 jutted out towards the British line as a menacing salient.

The front here had been established in the early days of the war. The French had been forced to concede Bapaume, then the flat land stretching towards the Pozières Ridge, fighting bitterly to hang on to the eastern slopes of the Ancre Valley until this position was also forced. They were then pushed relentlessly backwards until finally bringing the enemy's great advance to a halt, on a north-south line,

German transports moving up men in the region of Bapaume.

from Hannescamps, Foncquevillers and Hebuterne, down to the tiny hilltop village of Colincamps. The Germans' position left them looking over the very gently undulating Hebuterne-Colincamps plain, and they now dug themselves in, with every intention of holding this line. For the Germans now switched their efforts towards the east. The Schlieffen Plan had failed in its intention to produce a quick knockout blow and instead produced a state of stalemate. The Eastern Front, with its huge line, offered greater possibilities, and in any case the Russian Army was a far less formidably equipped military machine than its French counterpart. The German High Command was happy to hold positions more or less of its choice and let the allies throw themselves against them; for the French it was a matter of honour and an imperative to remove the Hun invader as soon as practicable.

See Map page 27 Yet the French attacked this line before Serre with some success, driving the Germans off the ridge, across the valley below, up through the four small stands of trees and forced them to alter the shape of their Front Line in this two thousand yard length. Now it curved down and around the front of the village, crossing the road coming into Serre from the south several hundred yards from the Heidenkopf, which now became a salient, a bulge in the German line, and a potentially vulnerable point.

The French took up their new positions with a contempt towards field fortifications. Not for them the fortress approach; they simply renamed the trenches vacated by the Germans in front of Serre. Fire steps were left on the wrong side and entrances to dugouts went unprotected, which was to lead to unnecessary casualties, for example, when the German artillery was turned upon their former barracks excavated under Toutvent Farm, now occupied by the French.

In January 1916 the disposition of the 52nd Division's three regiments was: the 170th Regiment (9th Baden) lay north of Serre and Puisieux, facing Hebuterne; below it the 66th Regiment (3rd Magdeburgers) was in front and just to the south of Puisieux; the 169th Regiment (8th Baden) occupied the village of Serre and on its left was the 121st Reserve Regiment (3rd Wurttemburgers).

In the spring of 1916, at full strength again after the battle with the French Second Army in the June of 1915, the 169th Regiment's front line was two thousand yards long with a notably strong defence system woven into and around Serre, taking full advantage of the ground and the ingenuity of the army's engineers. It resulted not only in a nigh on impregnable position, but also one in which the comfort and welfare of the troops were considered – not a matter that came high on the list of

Waiting to receive inoculations against typhus, German troops in the trenches at Serre. *Below*: **The village of Serre in German hands.**

priorities of their opponents. Serre's 'garrison' consisted of about two thousand four hundred men at full strength along with a heavy machine gun company. The men, divided into three battalions, would be aided if necessary by two companies, providing some four hundred men, from the 66th Regiment to the north and a further two companies

A section of German trench showing the type of constructions that had to be overcome by the attackers. Here steel girders are in evidence – the invaders were determined to stay put.

would be available from its southern flank from the 121st Reserve Regiment. Thus Serre could call upon a maximum of just under three and a half thousand men, with not less than ten heavy machine guns, occupying a most formidable array of defences whose task it would be to receive the assault of seven thousand British attacking uphill over open ground. The odds were stacked quite heavily on the side of the defenders, although if the attacking troops had enough artillery of the right sort and were able to adopt a flexible attack plan, there might be some hope of success.

In the last week of June 1916 the 169th Regiment, like so many other German units along the Somme front, was stunned by the most ferocious bombardment that it had yet faced. Yet despite the fact that the shells constantly fell on their lines and the village, their casualty list was surprisingly small, consisting of some two hundred dead, wounded and missing. Their strong defences and the lack of heavy British howitzers had played their part; perhaps the greatest damage was to the emotions and to morale as a never ending 'drumfire' fell on their positions for several days. Yet morale was kept high by the thought of what their own artillery fire was achieving on the much 'softer', less fortified British positions. It was likely that already the British casualties were far heavier than their own.

A German soldier makes some repairs to his kit. Note the steel plate with slot for rifle; this type of shield was placed on the parapet and afforded protection for a sniper.

The Regiment's twelve companies were disposed as follows on July 1st 1916: only four companies (4, 3, 6 and 7), some eight hundred men, occupied the first line of defences. Companies 1, 2, 8 and 5 were in the second and third lines, a further eight hundred men. Behind them in the village fortress line were three companies (9, 10 and 11). In the village itself and to its rear was the reserve company, 12.

On the left flank, occupying the Heidenkopf and facing two battalions of the Royal Warwickshire Regiment were two companies (2 and 3) of the 121st Reserve Regiment. These men had also suffered only minimal casualties, secure as they were in their deep dugouts; but the Germans realised the vulnerability of this salient position, jutting out from the rest of the German line. In the event the local commander, Major von Girunsee, was surprised by the unexpected

Skilful placing of machine guns ensured the failure of attacks in front of Serre. *Below:* **Maxim 08 on a wooden base; these were carried up from deep underground where they and their crews were safe from the British barrage prior to the attack on 1st July 1916.**

strength of the attack at the joint between the two British divisions, the 31st and the 4th, which was normally the weakest point of any onslaught. The attack on the Heidenkopf was one of the few British successes in this area on July 1st - and equally one of the few German misjudgements.

The ten heavy machine guns were the trump card in the German

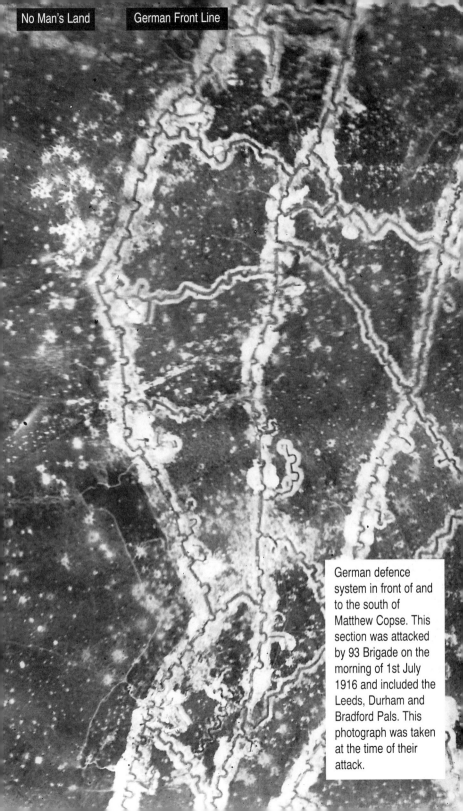

No Man's Land   German Front Line

German defence system in front of and to the south of Matthew Copse. This section was attacked by 93 Brigade on the morning of 1st July 1916 and included the Leeds, Durham and Bradford Pals. This photograph was taken at the time of their attack.

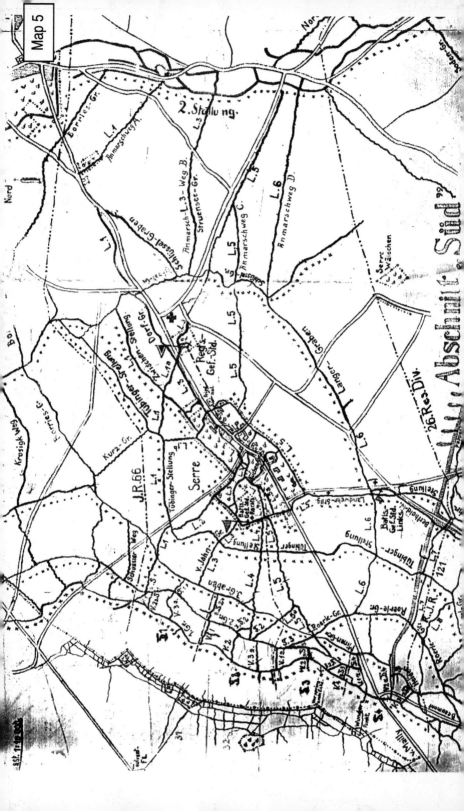

Map 5

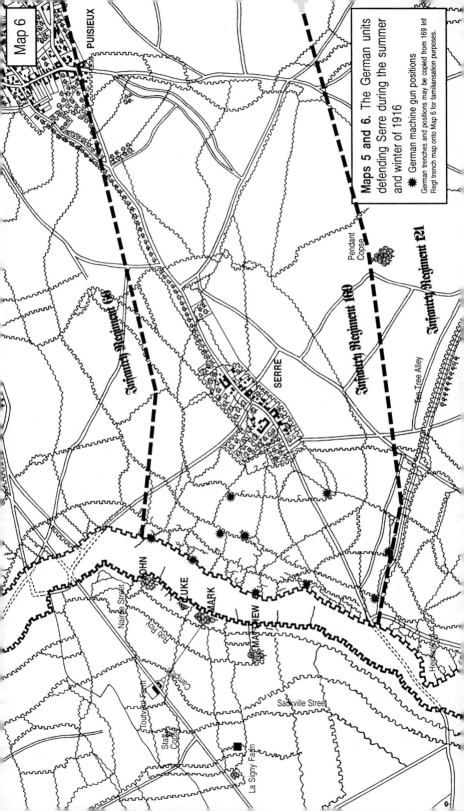

Map 6

PUISIEUX

Maps 5 and 6. The German units defending Serre during the summer and winter of 1916

✸ German machine gun positions

German trenches and positions may be copied from 169 Inf Regt trench map onto Map 6 for familiarisation purposes.

Infantry Regiment 66

Pendant Copse

SERRE

Infantry Regiment 169

Fen Tree Alley

Infantry Regiment 121

JOHN

Nairne Street

LUKE

Rob Roy

MARK

MATTHEW

Campbell Avenue

Toutvent Farm

Staff Copse

Sackville Street

Heidenkopf

La Signy Farm

defences; not just the guns themselves but the cunning and effective manner in which they were used. Over the twelve months since the German line had been altered by the French assault they had built great barriers of barbed wire, heavier than British wire, with longer points and a greater gauge. The barricades were arranged in patterns with V-shaped re-entrants, giving attacking infantry the illusion of avenues leading closer to the German trenches, and thereby would be moving straight into traps. The machine guns were sited to cover these enticing avenues, firing in enfilade across the front. Each gun post had a strongly built defence bulwark between the gunner and the attacker, making them very difficult targets for an increasingly desperate infantry. During any bombardment the machine guns and their operators were deep underground and safe from the shelling. Mounted on wooden 'skids' and with many months of practise they could be brought up and put in to action in less than two minutes.

Well hidden from the searching British artillery were the German guns, the lighter calibre ones in the deep winding clefts that lay between Serre and Miraumont.

The German defenders of the village at dawn on July 1st were ready to receive the British. They were stunned, deafened, frightened and exhausted by the bombardment, by the disruption to their rations and by the anticipation of the attack; but not, as yet, badly hurt.

German Artillery Brigade Headquarters on the Somme.

Chapter Four

THE DEATH OF ROLAND LEIGHTON

Apart from incessant labour, few events of importance occurred to either the 1/7th (c) or the 1/8th Battalion in the interval between Loos and the New Year.

(c) On November 7th Captain GS Tomkinson, then acting as Brigade Bombing Officer, was wounded by a rifle grenade. On December 23rd Lt RA Leighton, 1/7th Battalion was mortally wounded.

The Worcestershire Regiment in the Great War
Capt H Fitz M Stacke MC

Roland Leighton's name has been immortalised by the prominent impact he had on the life of Vera Brittain, whose fiance he was at the time of his death. She wrote her autobiography, and he features prominently in *Testament of Youth*, the first volume and which is readily available in print. It has been turned into a successful television series. The consequences of his death were to have a profound effect on her later life.

He was a member of 1/7 Worcesters, part of 144 Brigade (Gloucester and Worcester) of the 48th (South Midland) Division. They were among the first British troops to arrive in Picardy, an area of France in which few were destined not to serve over the next couple of years. A fellow member of 144 Brigade was 1/8th Worcesters; a member of the battalion, Edward Corbett, wrote a short but eloquent history of their war story in 1921, which describes the time in Hebuterne, *War Story of 1/8th (Territorial) Battalion, Worcestershire Regiment*. It gives a good sense of the atmosphere at this stage of the war.

'The first thing to do was to consolidate the trenches and prepare them for the winter, a prodigious and interminable task. All other things gave way to this. We all became sappers, the shovel was our weapon of war; we carried brickbats instead of bombs; and the sandbag became our oriflamme. In fact, one wretched soldier, who, while resting had dared to cover his wet legs with two of them, was told by an infuriated Brigadier that a sandbag was worth more than a man.' He noted that the main task of soldiers for the war was not fighting, engaging in attacks or even enduring bombardments, but rather, 'incessant toil and bodily discomfort. The gentlemen at home who strike for an eight hour day or forty odd hour working week can scarcely realise that for months on end we worked anything from twelve to twenty four hours a day, never had a bed to sleep on, furniture of any kind, houses to live in, seldom a decent roof over our heads and hardly ever dry clothes, and that we throve on it. The health, vigour and joviality of all ranks throughout these terrible winters were amazing. Cases of sickness were almost unknown, pleurisy and pneumonia did not occur. The chief enemies to our health were vermin and trench foot.

'The former was a legacy from our gallant Allies. We did not know what they were – one remembers a gallant Sergeant surveying with wonder seventeen corpses laid out on the parapet – but we learned: oh yes, we learned. If you get well bitten by these creatures you acquire trench fever which is very like malaria, but far more painful... for those who had to bear it, it was terrible: the loathing, the incessant bodily pain which on the march became agony, and the feeling of indignity, these were unbearable.

'Trench foot was a great puzzle to soldiers, and still greater to the Medical Corps, but to the alluvial miner it is an old friend.

'It arises from checked circulation in wet feet. So long as your feet are free they can endure harmlessly any amount of damage - they are designed to do so. But wrap tight puttees around your legs, draw your tight socks over your feet, get both shrunken with wet and in two days or so your feet will simply die. The cure of a bad case takes several months and is very expensive and the pain is terrible. The prevention is quite simple – hot drinks and bare feet for half an hour or so once a day. We adopted this plan, and in the winter of 1915-16 had only one case – a man with very poor circulation.

'August was warm, with heavy thunderstorms. The trenches were flooded, and it was a pretty sight to see a company filing along *sans* all clothing but shirts and boots. September was a glorious summer month, in the middle of which we took up our billets at Bus-les-Artois, a big village with a fine manor house, which was Divisional Headquarters. Here we wintered, and very comfortable we were.

'We had barns well supplied with hay to live in and sleep in, and the first thing was to put them in repair. Barns in Picardy are made of wattle and daub over a fine framework of oak; nearly every house has one, and they are often of enormous size. We could get no tools from the Sappers, no tools nor even nails. We made our tools (except a saw which was beyond us until we picked up a gunner's saw in the road), got nails from the ration boxes, and used the ration boxes and biscuit tins for patching and furnishing until they were required for building the horse lines. Mending the walls was easy; we found suitable clay and puddled it, and stole wattle from the wood, and for the roofs we picked up fallen tiles. All of this was typical of the service. We were ordered to repair billets and refused all tools and material; indeed we were forbidden to scrounge the latter. But we did the work and we did it well.' He notes that things became very quiet in the sector in the autumn, with the great battle of Loos raging in the north. 'Our artillery activity was limited to six rounds a day in each sector. The enemy could only reply with three, which he always handed to us at tea time. Our gunners were forbidden to fire any more without the leave of the CRA [Commander, Royal Artillery]; and if he was away when required the opportunity was lost.' 'Summer ended with a full gale and torrents of rain on Michaelmas Day, and till the next April we never saw a dry road or picked up stick or stone that was not wet. Life was one long struggle with the elements. The unrevetted trench walls tumbled in, the lower trenches were flooded, the wretched billets at Hebuterne became shower baths, our clothes, our blankets were always sodden. The unrelenting toil was doubled.

'In October we got some ammunition and lashed the enemy lines with a terrible bombardment – forty rounds. A few nights later he suffered a panic and for hours directed an intense musketry and machine gun fire on our lines and the landscape generally.

'After this he got shells and Hebuterne became a very lively place.

'One notable gun – a 10 inch naval gun which travelled along the railway to the east – made things especially hot for us.

'And all the time his fortifications were growing – not in our haphazard undirected way, when one regiment destroyed what its predecessor had done, to have its own work altered by the next – but on a definite, able plan, admirably planned and sedulously carried out. We watched Serre grow to a stronghold with terrible Gommecourt as a bastion on the right and the Quadrilateral to the German left. It looked to be impregnable and proved to be so, for it was never taken.

'Both sides were too busy to fight much, and the artillery had all the sport. The Reports called it "artillery duels". The term suggests two guns firing at each other; but in those days it implied an unlimited number of guns strafing each other's infantry (and sometimes their own). Neither side fired at each other's transport.

'The enemy's convoys used to go along the skyline into Serre, and we used to march in broad daylight and full view of Serre and Gommecourt to and from the trenches. Not till the Battle of the Somme caused both sides to lose their tempers and engendered bad blood were these courtesies abandoned. At any rate our food was safe.'

It was during the winter of 1915 that Roland Leighton became a part of what was termed trench wastage – one of the unfortunate few who got picked off during a routine tour in the trenches.

Below is the account of his death and funeral sent by Robert Leighton (his father) to Vera Brittain.

'The trenches which the 7th Worcesters entered for the first time on 22nd December had been occupied previously by the Oxford [sic] Regt, who had left them in a very bad condition. Roland's platoon were to spend the night in them and, while doing so, were to repair the wire entanglements. He had been in the dug-out, **K**, most of the evening, and had his supper there. He left the dug-out at 11.30 and went back to the officers' trench quarters, where he saw Colonel Harman and got his men together to go out to do his work on the wire.

'The line **M** represents the direction in which he led his men, making a detour eastward to avoid the enemy's possible fire and then creeping along the shadowed side of the hedge **B** towards the point **F**, where a temporary plank bridge was flung across the flooded trench. Here he halted his platoon and went in advance to show the way and select the spots to be mended.

'The red line [top one in diagram] represents the German fire trench, divided from the English trench (blue) [thick line below it] by about a hundred yards of riven ground. This ground slopes downwards from **A** towards the enemy's lines.

'**s. s** and **e. e** are sap and communication trenches.

'**H** is the wire entanglements which especially needed repair. The **X** marks the spot where Roland fell.

'**K** is the signallers' dug-out, where Captain Adam posted half a dozen of his men to cover and protect the wiring party. Adam was still here when the Germans opened fire from **G** towards **H** and **F**. He ordered his men to fire and divert the enemy's aim from the wiring party.

'One of Roland's men came running towards **K** and calling out: "Mr Leighton is hit." The firing was continued. Adam ran out towards **F**, crossed the trench after Sergeant Day and found Roland at **X** lying on his face, unable to move his body or lower limbs, but moving his

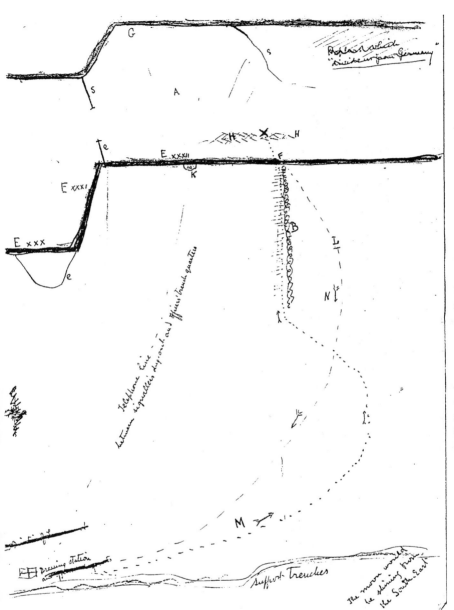

arms and turning his face around to see who was coming. He knew both the sergeant and Captain Adam. He said to Adam: "Its got me in the stomach." Adam and the sergeant at once turned him over on his back and Adam said "I think it's lower down." Roland said "I know my stomach has got it – badly." Adam then said: "Well, we'll soon get it out", and, kneeling beside him, he added: "Put your arms round my neck and hold on whilst I lift you." Roland did so, clasping his hands together and making an effort to raise himself. The sergeant helped to lift and, with Adam, carried him, under fire, back to the point **F** and into the shelter of the trench, where the platoon had been halted. A bearer ran off for the stretcher and to act as guide to the doctor, while another stretcher bearer began to apply first aid. This second bearer was shot in the thigh while working.

'Adam, meanwhile, ran back to the dug-out and telephoned to the dressing station for the doctor, who was there with the Colonel.

'Captain Adam returned at once to **F** and presently the doctor came, followed by the stretcher bearer. The doctor got Roland out of the trench and on to the stretcher which was carried along the south side of the hedge to the point marked **L**. The enemy were still firing obliquely in this direction as well as towards the dug-out. It was at **L** that Dr Sheridan took his first opportunity to inject morphia and staunch the bleeding. Roland then repeated: "It's got me in the stomach." Until then he was in agony, obviously agitated and anxious, but very brave. In the moonlight they saw that his lips were firm pressed, his eyes very wide open and his face pale. He did not seem to wish to speak. He did not moan, even when moved. He appeared to understand what the doctor was doing with the needle. The morphia at once deadened the pain.

'**N** is the line of the direction taken by the stretcher bearers to the dressing station. It was during this journey that he "kept up a conversation" with the doctor. But Captain Adam declares that it was all incoherent – the mere remnants of what had been in his mind just before he was struck.

'Roland's servant, McHugh, had been in the dug-out all this time.

'He had heard the cry: "Mr Leighton is hit." He wanted to go to him, but remained until ordered to go out and help carry the wounded stretcher bearer to the dressing station.

'When Colonel Harman and the doctor received Captain Adam's telephone message, they telephoned at once to Louvencourt for the motor ambulance, and it arrived at the dressing station before Dr Sheridan had plugged up the wounds and applied a more careful dressing.

'Dr Sheridan alone accompanied the ambulance to the hospital and he agreed with Colonel Barling that Roland was too weak from internal shock to be operated upon before morning.

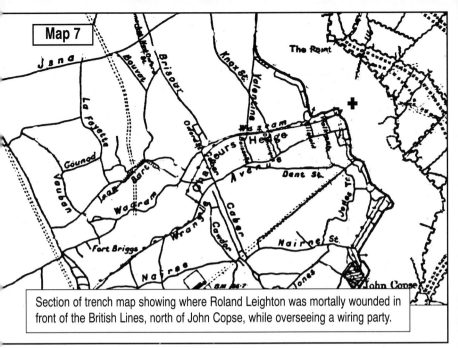

Section of trench map showing where Roland Leighton was mortally wounded in front of the British Lines, north of John Copse, while overseeing a wiring party.

'At the funeral the chief mourners were Colonel Harman, Colonel Barling, Captain Sheridan and Captain Adam. McHugh was also present. Men could not be spared from the trenches to form a firing party, but in other respects it was a military field funeral, very solemn, very simple, very beautiful. The mourners were all impressed by the sudden breaking forth of the sun as they followed the coffin out of the church and along the road to the cemetery. The acolite [sic] who carried the censer was a picturesque figure. Incense was wafted into the grave. Holy water was sprinkled....'

One of Roland Leighton's (1895 - 1915) poems was entitled *Vale*:

> *And so farewell. All our sweet songs are sung,*
> *Our re-rose garlands withered:*
> *The sun-bright day –*
> *Silver and blue and gold –*
> *Wearied to sleep.*
>
> *The shimmering evening, like a grey, soft bird,*
> *Barred with the blood of sunset,*
> *Has flown to rest*
> *Under the scented wings*
> *Of the dark-blue Night.*

1/8th Worcesters spent a short while in the line before Serre, prior to being relieved by 31st Division.

'We remained here till the beginning of April, losing 9 killed and 27 wounded, some of them by the fire of the guns of 31st Division, which had relieved our old comrades of the 4th on our right. It was not, perhaps, the fault of the gunners so much as the very untrustworthy American shells which were then in use.'

'The worst of the place [Serre] was the awful gloom that even on a sunny day hung about the deep grim trenches. One felt it everywhere. Our astrologer said that it came from the ghosts of the old battle waiting to escort away the ghosts of a future fight – a prophecy that had a frightful fulfilment.'

> *Goodbye, sweet friend, what matters it that you*
> *Have found Love's death in joy and I in sorrow?*
> *For hand in hand, just as we used to do,*
> *We too shall live our passionate poem through*
> *On God's serene tomorrow.*
> **Roland Leighton**

Chapter Five

THE DEATH OF INNOCENCE
The Second Battle for Serre, 1st July 1916

The 31st Division, comprising three brigades of infantry of which ten battalions were recruited from Yorkshire (eleven if the Pioneer battalion is included), one from Lancashire and one from Durham, was part of Fourth Army commanded by Lieut Gen Sir Henry Rawlinson. His Army would fight the initial stages of the first British Battle of the Somme.

The origins of the Battle of the Somme, its strategic objectives and the complications created by the planning of a huge offensive by two allies are not part of this book. Let it suffice to say that the planning was meticulous, the efforts to provide an infrastructure for the rear areas to cope with the massive influx of men and material extraordinary, with the most comprehensive system ever so far arranged for the evacuation of the wounded. Yet the planning was often flawed, the scheme, once launched, could not be easily changed and the extent of the casualties overwhelmed the evacuation system, at least on the first day of this battle that went on for over four and a half months. Added to this was the lack of experience of many of the divisions involved and their supporting artillery – soldiers, company officers, battalion commanders, brigadiers, divisional commanders and beyond, as well as their staffs. They had been in the army long enough – but had not yet faced the anvil of fire and battle which would beat them into the fine fighting force that army became as a consequence of the bloody lessons learned on the fields of the Somme.

The division at Serre was at the northern point of the whole fifteen mile British offensive line; it would sweep around in an arc of ninety degrees and provide a shield from German attacks from the north as the rest of the army pivoted upon it and swept the Germans off their heights, out of the Ancre and beyond, with the cavalry ready to follow in hot pursuit. This northernmost division would have one hour and fifty minutes to perform its task and to establish its shield, and end up facing north, retaining its link with 48th (South Midland) Division to its left.

31st Division's right flank ran along the front of the four small copses, with the most northerly one, John, precisely at the division's –

49

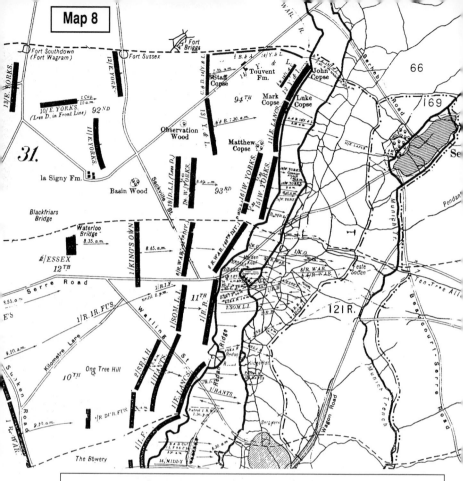

Official History Map showing the disposition of the 31st Division on the extreme north of the Somme attack. This meant that the German 66 Regiment, with no assault on their front to contend with, could concentrate their defensive fire on the attackers to their left and thus enfilade the Pals Battalions' assault.

indeed the army's – pivot point. Beyond this copse there would be no battle other than a diversionary attack at Gommecourt, two miles further to the north. The northerly barricade that the division was to create was to be three thousand yards long, stretching eastwards from John Copse.

The task given to the division involved a most complex military manoeuvre, all of which had to be achieved under the fire of an extremely able enemy which had had many months both to fortify the ground on which it stood and also to know the ground over which its

Above: Recruits for the 1st Barnsley Pals (13th Battalion York & Lancaster Regiment) on one of their early parades – no uniforms available at this stage – drawn mainly from the collieries in the town area.
Below: City Battalion men (12th Batt York & Lancaster Regt) at their hutted camp on the moors outside Sheffield. They were, for the most part, office workers.

'I'll always remember the Sheffielders with their handerkerchiefs stuffed up their sleeves and their wristwatches flashing in the sun. They were the elite of Sheffield. We were the ragged arse battalion but they were the coffee and bun boys.'

Pte Frank Lindley
2nd Barnsley Pals

enemy was coming, and to register (that is to establish accurately the range) targets for its artillery. The infantry of 31st Division was composed entirely of 'Pals'.

The Pals phenomenon, one feels, could only have come about in Great Britain. This was a country that had for many years, perhaps for good reason, neglected its army to the benefit of its navy. When entanglement in continental war came about in 1914 the machine was totally inadequate to produce the sort of manpower that the new War Minister, Kitchener, realised would be required to win that war. In a characteristic solution, men from many towns and cities (chiefly in the great northern industrial towns), were recruited under local control, generally the town councils. They were trained in local parks, housed in municipal buildings, clothed and equipped by the town and often officered by local worthies and a number of 'dugouts' from previous conflicts, most notably the Boer War at the turn of the century. After some months they were inspected by the War Office, found to be 'efficient' and taken over by the army, the town being compensated for its expenditure[1]. Although they were given battalion numbers according to the Regiment to which they were attached (with the addition of 'Service' to their battalion number) the vast majority retained their nicknames – Hull Commercials, Sheffield City, Barnsley, Bradford, Accrington and Leeds Pals. After a period of training, often on Salisbury Plain, they were despatched overseas, some to Egypt, but most to France. Even those that went to Egypt, like the 31st Division, soon returned to France. Many of them had been in the army for eighteen months or more before they fought on 1st July – a long time to be in training. But they were all so inexperienced, as were their staff officers, their artillery and their support arms a striking contrast to the Germans opposite, with a war machine based on a complex and intensive conscription programme that had existed ever since the foundation of the Second Reich in 1870.

The Battle of the Somme of 1916 was to be the first time that most of Kitchener's Army would face a major battle, an inferno of fire and steel. The one thing that they brought to the battle was the most tremendous elan and loyalty to each other; they were pals. It may be something that we cannot understand now, or which the more intellectually inclined would find ridiculous, but the fact was that they were, and that was how they intended to fight. And this was a division of Pals.

It has been argued that the division was given this task at Serre because the task would be easy, and afterwards all they would have to do was establish and hold a new line. It is true that the very smallness of the small village, with what seemed to be an insubstantial defensive system, did not present an impossible task. This outward appearance belied the hidden strength of the German fortress that had been created over the months since the French attack ended in June 1915. The problem was probably well appreciated by the staff. They relied, principally, on the overwhelming artillery bombardment to smash

Men of the Royal Warwicks moving up to the Front on the Somme.

these military works and which would also shatter the morale and ability to resist of the defenders. They were also, and this was certainly true at divisional level, confident in the outstanding comradeship that had been built up in the division since the early months of the war.

To the left of 31st Division, the 48th would stage diversionary fire on their front, though they 'lent' half of 143 Brigade to their neighbour. These two battalions, Territorials of the Royal Warwickshire Regiment (1/6th and 1/8th) were put at the joint between 31st Division and 4th Division to its immediate south, or right.

From the corner of John Copse down to the right hand man of 1/8th Warwicks was a front line of 2,000 yards, with fifteen battalions confronting this insignificant little ridge top village. Four of these battalions were from Hull, comprising 92 Bde, which would be in reserve on the day, 800 to 1500 yards behind the front line, entrenched on the Hebuterne-Colincamps Plain and just over the western edge of the shallow valley in the battle arena. In that valley, on both sides of it, were 93 and 94 Brigades, those of 31st Division that would attack.

From north to south, the first 800 yards of front ran along the eastern edge of the four copses, with the remainder of the division's front being in the open, 300 yards above the valley floor.

In the front line, starting from John Copse, were half the Barnsley men of 14/Y&L, then Sheffield City men (12/Y&L). Beyond them were the Accrington Pals (11/East Lancs) and on their right were the Leeds Pals (15/West Yorks) who were adjacent to the Warwicks. In the front line trench and the five deep saps cut from it and under No Man's Land were strong elements from the four companies of 12/KOYLI, Miners and Pioneers' from Leeds.

Behind these front line troops, again commencing from the north, in company waves of one hundred yards distance, were the other half of 14/Y&L. 1st Barnsley Pals (13/Y&L) were to the rear of the Lancashire men from Accrington. To the right of them were 16/West Yorks from Bradford, in trenches to the rear of the Leeds Pals. The right hand man of the Leeds Pals could shake hands with the left hand man of 1/8th Warwicks. A hundred yards behind 16/West Yorks were their fellow Bradford men of 18/West Yorks. Behind both of these battalions were 18/DLI, but D Company of the Geordies had been placed further forward, on the right flank of 16/West Yorks. All the battalions of both brigades were staggered in hundred yard waves throughout and on both sides of the shallow valley. The dispositions were planned to take into account the nature of the manoeuvre that was expected of the division - the fewest troops at the point of the pivot, the weight of manpower increasing towards the end of the sweeping arm.

Dispersed amongst all the battalions in both brigades were 12/KOYLI (T'owd Twelfth) mainly miners and many from Charlesworth Pit who had streamed into Leeds from the surrounding villages in 1914. Whole shifts marched together to enlist, shepherded in by regular sergeants in uniform who coaxed others out of pubs as they went, until eventually arriving at the railway station to be put on board trains taking them into Farnley Camp at Otley. These men's heroic but unsung task was to suffer the annihilating bombardment and machine gun fire of the Germans whilst rebuilding shattered trenches and bridges and keeping the communication trenches clear of the awful obstructions brought about by the ferocious weight of the shelling. They had to bring out the wounded, clear those who had died and bury many on the spot on the trench floor. They had to fetch and carry barbed wire, stakes, water, food and anything that was needed by the infantrymen, such as ammunition, grenades and mortar bombs – the whole without any opportunity of their own to have a go at the enemy.

The westward edge of the valley was topped with a long track running due north from the ruins of the large La Signy Farm to a point five hundred yards behind John Copse, where it dipped down into the flat land that lay before Hebuterne. Roughly half way along this track was Observation Copse, in front of which a ten foot deep dugout had been made to hold the brigade headquarters, giving the staff a view over the whole of the division's battlefield and also of their objective,

Infantry Regiments at Serre
31st (PALS) DIVISION

Major General R Wanless O'Gowan

92 Brigade

10th Battalion East Yorkshire **Hull Commercials**	11th Battalion East Yorkshire **Hull Tradesmen**	12th Battalion East Yorkshire **Hull Sportsmen**	13th Battalion East Yorkshire **Hull T'others**

93 Brigade

15th Battalion West Yorkshire **Leeds Pals**	16th Battalion West Yorkshire **1st Bradford**	18th Battalion West Yorkshire **2nd Bradford**	18th Battalion Durham LI **Durham Pals**

94 Brigade

12th Battalion York & Lancs **Sheffield City**	13th Battalion York & Lancs **1st Barnsley**	14th Battalion York & Lancs **2nd Barnsley**	11th Battalion East Lancs **Accrington Pals**

12th Battalion Kings Own Yorks LI **Leeds Miners**

1/6th Royal Warwicks
1/8th Royal Warwicks

the ruins of Serre. They could also appreciate the external strength of the German position, approximately 800 yards away, its trenches and barbed wire forest. The artillery would doubtless put paid to that. Of the extent of the German underground position they had only the haziest notion.

To the left rear of this position, about 500 yards away, was Staff Copse (both these names a direct translation from the original French trench maps). Directly behind Luke Copse, also sitting alongside the track, were the ruins of the large Toutvent Farm, reduced to a pile of bricks and strewn detritus. The valley below was interlaced with trenches, all given names such as Monk, Eczema, Rob Roy, Nairne, Copse, Flag and Campion to name but a few. From these trenches long communication trenches were dug out of the valley, stretching westwards. Some of them had entrances 2,000 yards away, close to the road running north from Colincamps to Hebuterne. Coming south eastwards from the ridge top track near La Signy Farm was a long trench, Sackville Street. It was effectively 31st Division's right hand boundary, though it passed through both battalions of the Royal Warwicks. Just beyond its commencement a military police post was set up at Red Cottage to control the movements of troops in and out of the battle area. In front of the farm was a small round wood sprouting out of a hollow, Basin Wood. A large pit had been dug there to accommodate the dead from the forthcoming battle, a daunting and sobering sight for troops moving up for the attack.

31st Division had arrived in the Serre area in April 1916 on its arrival in France from a time spent in Egypt guarding the Suez Canal approaches. The base was about five miles away to the west around Bus-les-Artois. Most of its 15,000 men would have made constant treks in and out of the front, taking their turn to hold the line, to dig and improve the position, to rebury many of the hastily covered French dead as they did so and to make the trench system one from which a major attack could be launched.

They had two months to familiarise themselves with this new territory; two months when they faced an enemy for the first time; two months to learn their task in the forthcoming 'Big Push'. They had very little idea of what the German line looked like, though there were maps and aerial photographs from which to work. To spend too long gazing eastwards was to invite retribution from an alert enemy.

The German opposition had been at Serre for twenty months now. Unlike the British who were forced to move troops from sector to sector, especially as the army mushroomed in size, the Germans were almost static. They had built their defences with care and consideration; their men had ample opportunity to know exactly how to react to attack. They had time to make their men as comfortable as possible – a contrast to their adversary.

The Germans could also view the preparations the British were making, both from here and from the high ground which lay behind their front line. Their artillery was well concealed and could register the British positions; whilst much of the British artillery (the vast proportion of which was light and therefore short range) was often positioned on the open plain.

All was not quiet even before the fateful day. Constant interrupting artillery fire and patrolling reaped its crop of dead and wounded Pals. On 18th June, for example, an estimated 150 6" shells fell on the 200 yards of front line trench in John Copse in the space of one hour. Amongst those who were buried for ever was Company Sergeant Major Marsden, a big, genial man.

The battle was originally to start on 29th June; from Saturday 24th the artillery was going to batter the German defences into ruins, particularly the wire, and destroy the German defenders as effective fighting troops. Huge stock piles of ammunition had been brought forward (no easy task) and hundreds of guns would set about their task. Almost two thirds of these were field artillery, 18 pounders, whose

High explosive howitzer shells being brought to the guns.

Loading a 9.2 inch howitzer at the start of the Somme Battle.

main task was to destroy the barbed wire defences; over three hundred howitzers would destroy machine gun posts and trenches, whilst the heaviest artillery was dedicated to destroying the deep, strong dugouts and underground barracks. Almost two million shells were fired along the front of the battle.

There was a well thought out artillery plan, but observation, so vital to effective artillery fire, was hampered by the very poor weather. This denied observation to the artillery observation officers on the ground of the damage that was being caused, whilst for the same reason static balloons and aerial observation were rendered useless or impossible. Counter-battery work, that is the targeting and destruction of the enemy artillery, was also made difficult, especially as many German batteries remained silent and therefore unobserved, saving their efforts until the attack had been launched. The rain also flooded trenches, breaking down their walls and making those in the valley particularly difficult to use.

Despite all of this, preparations had to continue; endless lines of men brought up ammunition, mortar bombs, grenades, water and all the paraphernalia of war. Men were rotated from the front to undergo training in the rear over mock-ups of the German lines that had been laid out by the Royal Engineers. Besides this, trenches had to be manned, patrols went out to check on the effectiveness of the bombardment and to try and capture prisoners to determine the state of morale of the Germans; and they had to carry up heavy kit. To add to their exhaustion, long marches had to be made to the safer areas in the rear – and all of this in the possible confusion of the communication trenches, themselves often obstructed with signals wire which had come adrift or had been damaged by shell fire. The strain was considerable. To compound this atmosphere the Germans also patrolled vigorously – and they had had many months of active service to sharpen their technique and efficiency.

On the morning of 28th June the attack was postponed from Z day because of the restrictions imposed by the weather and the need for more work to be done on the wire. The attack was now to be launched at 7.30 am on 1st July. The Germans sat and waited, seeing some of their defences smashed to ruin and suffering some, but surprisingly few, casualties. Their artillery bombarded the British positions – infantry and artillery, but the modest volume of this fire deceived their enemy. The concealed batteries patiently waited for their moment.

During the evening of 30th June those battalions which had been detailed for the attack made their long march of five to seven miles into the trenches, across fields soaked in water and deep in the cloying mud of the Somme, entering crowded and narrow communications trenches whose floors were in a semiliquid condition. Caked in mud and tired out, the men got into their positions between 2 and 4 am, carrying their heavy loads of kit, emergency rations, spare ammunition and grenades, weapons, entrenching tools, wire cutters and often reels of barbed wire and other trench stores. But they were in a high state of anticipation, buoyed up at the thought that something was going to happen and encouraged by the ferocious sound of their artillery bombardment.

The four battalions of the East Yorks from Hull which had been holding the divisional front, patrolling, cutting wire and suffering casualties now withdrew out of the valley and beyond the La Signy-Touvent farms ridge, doubtless grateful to be spared the advance into the unknown in a few hours time. Two of their platoons remained with 18/DLI and 70 men went to the Accrington Pals as reinforcements. All knew what their task was in the carefully worked out plan; it was not so clear what was to happen if the plan went wrong.

31st Division had a hundred and ten minutes to establish their new defensive line from the moment that the attack commenced. It had to smash through four lines of deep German trenches and their thick barbed wire defences as well as overcoming the ten heavy machine guns of which they had limited knowledge. Bradford and Durham men on the right flank would have to advance 3,000 yards, with the outer flank having to hold Pendant Wood on the edge of Ten Tree Alley. The Royal Warwicks were to remove the Heidenkopf, the bulge in the German line and thereby ease their progress.

Shells falling on the German front lines prior to the attack. The barrage on the front line would fall silent at about the same time that the huge Hawthorn mine, two miles to the south of Serre, was exploded under the German strongpoint known as the Hawthorn Redoubt – *Right.*

13 and 14/Y&L, 18/West Yorks and 18/DLI would then leapfrog as those who had gone ahead succeeded, consolidating positions and eliminating pockets of enemy resistance. They would be followed by the Hull brigade, whilst the Pioneers would connect German trenches to the British and effect emergency repairs. The Germans would then be confronted by a well dug in division, elated by victory and prepared to deal with the inevitable counter attacks from Puisieux.

At 6.30 am the tempo of the British artillery increased, pouring fire on the German front; this lasted for fifty minutes. The weather had turned and the morning was clear and sunny. The Germans were clear about when the assault was going to happen from a variety of intelligence sources. They had managed to fly two balloons on 30th June and could appreciate fully the significance of the thousands of men that were flooding into the area. Their concealed artillery could now come into its own, launching a devastating fire on the comparatively soft British line, their guns already accurately laid for the task. The soldiers in the British front could only hug the trench walls and floors, suffer considerable casualties and wait for the off.

At 7.20 am several things happened almost simultaneously. A great British mine was blown under Hawthorn Redoubt, about two miles to the south of Serre. At this moment the artillery barrage was lifted from the German front line – a clear and distinct signal to the battered

Germans that now was the moment. Half companies of the five leading battalions climbed out of their trenches and ran forward a hundred yards, lying down in front of the enemy wire and, with luck, out of range of German hand grenades. Stokes Mortars located in the saps that had been dug out just below the surface into No Man's Land now broke out from their overhead cover and began to let loose a barrage of 3,000 rounds onto the enemy front line trench. The final ingredient in this series of events was the letting off of an ineffectual smoke screen by 48th Division on the left, which drifted over onto the ground over which the Sheffield City Battalion would advance.

Within a few minutes the British bombardment resumed its incessant fire, but concentrated further to the rear – this entirely the case for the heavier pieces of artillery. The 18 pounders, firing shrapnel, raised their sights to the German second line wire. At 7.25 am the second half of the forward companies came out of their trenches and ran forward fifty yards, then lay down and awaited zero

L o g e a s t   P u i s i e u x — a u — M o r

This panoramic view was taken from Basin Wood, 12th April, 1916. The 31st Division attacked from the left (the line of broken trees is one of the copses – possibly Mark) towards Serre on the right opposite.

hour.

The enemy were now relieved from the storm of shells they had endured for the past week. They were amazed that the enemy had come out into the open and were preparing to attack at the same time as their artillery had left them without support. The Germans redoubled their own shelling of the British front and No Man's Land. Their machine gunners and riflemen took up their positions, ignoring the relatively light shrapnel and mortar gun fire and made the most of the tempting targets that the infantry presented before them.

At 7.30 am the whistles blew and the rest of the troops came out of their trenches to follow those already in No Man's Land; at a steady walk they headed for the gaps cut in the British wire and expected to be able to continue this progress across the, supposedly cut, German wire and onto their objectives. Those in the following battalions began their advance to the front as well; they came in long files, the better to cross the many trenches between them and the Germans. As those on the left came forward they could see that the fog created by the smoke candles had drifted across our leading men and which now served to obscure the sight of their objectives.

The British barrage was now falling some hundreds of yards ahead of the leading infantry. The time scale of the advance was so tight that this, the forerunner of all creeping barrages, required the advancing infantry to maintain a steady speed to retain its protection. Already

Serre ———— _Bihucourt Church_

they were falling well behind.

The control of the conduct of the battle had now moved from the Generals and even the battalion commanders, who were instructed to remain in the trenches in the first phase of the attack. This meant that it was junior officers and NCOs who were commanding the advance; and it was in just this category of soldier that Kitchener's Army was most deficient – the well tried and tested NCO who would have had time to train the junior officers. The men who had worked so hard to bring their battalions to a peak of battle readiness were now left – supposing they had survived – to watch their worst nightmare taking place in front of them in reality.

The artillery had tried very hard to carry out the vital part of the plan that was their's. The shrapnel used for the most part by the field artillery was inadequate for the task of breaking up the German wire - it was not until the introduction of the instantaneous fuse that this particular problem was considerably overcome. A shortage of heavy calibre guns meant that many of the German underground shelters were untouched. Poor visibility in the early stages of the attack had not helped, nor had the excessively high proportion of dud rounds – perhaps as high as thirty percent of all those fired. Only where the artillery was heavy enough and of the right quality (on the British sector, only at Montauban) did it do its job; and there the attack succeeded.

On the left of the attack, 14/Y&L were pushed to the right by the long range machine gun and artillery fire coming from the edge of Rossignol Wood, and in to the path of 12/Y&L. The men were knocked down in droves as they began to bunch and searched in vain for gaps in the German wire. The Sheffield Pals in their turn wandered to their right, a few finding a gap in the wire and surged into the front line trench. The Accringtons headed straight towards the village and were mown down by the sustained heavy machine gun fire, yet some of these too found their way into the German line.

Further on the right the fortunes of 93 Bde were no better. The Leeds Pals were almost destroyed as a fighting force for that day before they even went over the top, and even those who had been in No Man's Land before zero hour failed to make any impact on the German line. Behind them the 1st Bradford Pals met a similar dreadful fate, making their approach over the very open ground in which they were entrenched. Within half an hour from the commencement of the assault over two thousand men were down, either wounded in No Man's Land or dead. The German barbed wire had held the troops at bay and their artillery and machine guns had done the rest. Battalion commanders in the front could see that the battle was lost; whilst their beloved battalions could never again be what they had been. The Pals ideal was being destroyed before their eyes.

At 9.30 am 18/DLI, 800 yards from the front line, stuck to their schedule even though they could see the awful disaster spread out before them. They went over the top in file, passing through 2nd Bradfords who had gone before them, with what was left of that battalion sheltering as best they could. They would get no further than the ruined forward trenches of 93 Bde. On the left 1st Barnsley Pals had made a similar approach to the front, and also took their place in the disastrous scheme of things.

Meanwhile the surviving members of the detached element of 18/DLI, D Company, on the right hand edge of 1st Bradfords (16/West Yorks), continued to go forward into the smoke-shrouded battlefield, somehow surviving the numerous geysers of earth and shrapnel blown skywards by the enemy shells. The small metal plates made from pieces of biscuit tin and fastened to their back packs glistened in the sunshine and showed, to the observers in the rear and to the aircraft above, the Geordies' progress. Their progress was monitored as they moved further and further forward, diminishing in numbers as they went. It was reported that a dozen had penetrated the incredible distance of 2,000 yards until they reached the ridge top Pendant Copse and disappeared from view altogether – and forever.

31st Division's assault had come to a sanguinary halt; the fear now was that the Germans would counter-attack, and with enemy fire

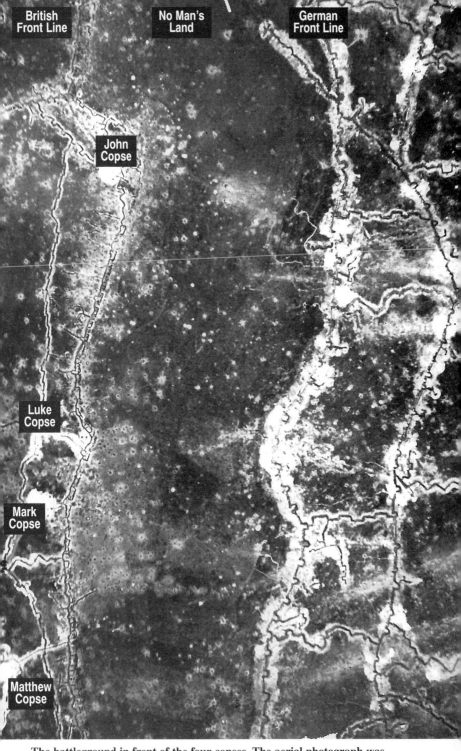

British
Front Line

No Man's
Land

German
Front Line

John
Copse

Luke
Copse

Mark
Copse

Matthew
Copse

The battleground in front of the four copses. The aerial photograph was
taken on the morning of the attack by an aircraft of the RFC.

showing no sign of abating the Hull battalions of 92 Bde were left in their reserve position.

Further south the Birmingham Territorials, 1/8th and 1/6th Warwicks, had also set off at 7.30 am. With the 1/8th in the lead they had swarmed over the slight rise in front of them, crossed the Serre Road and battered their way through the German fortress of the Heidenkopf. With 1/6th close behind them they fought their way for a thousand yards into what should have been 31st Division's right

The German strongpoint known as the *Heidenkopf* which thrust out as a salient into No Man's Land. The Territorials of the Warwickshire Regiment, 1/6th and 1/8th, managed to fight their way into this heavily defended stronghold.

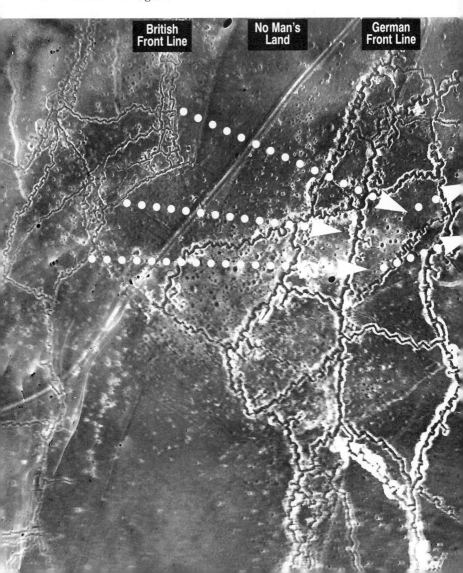

boundary, 600 yards south of the village and crossed the junction of the German trench system at Munich Trench and Ten Tree Alley with the trench leading to Beaucourt. However the experienced Germans of the tough 169th Infantry Regiment, relieved of the necessity to defend Serre because of the destruction of 31st Division, rushed reinforcements to the area. The Warwicks were left in the air by the failure of the units on either side, those of the 31st and 4th Divisions. They had crossed two of the German lines and in just thirty minutes had reached the German third line of defence and were attempting to consolidate their gain. They were ejected and fought their way back in again on several occasions. Behind 1/6th Warwicks were trying to reach them but were being held up by the impenetrable German artillery fire, so that in the end only a few made it.

As the day progressed into afternoon supplies of bombs and ammunition began to run dangerously short. There was no alternative but to retire, leaving their dead and many of their wounded behind them. About ten hours after they had set off, they found themselves back where they had started, a shadow of their former selves. 1/8th had lost their CO, Lieutenant-Colonel E A Innes killed, and 21 out of the 23 officers who had gone over the top were killed or wounded, with only one taken prisoner because he was too badly injured to move. The total casualties of the battalion on that terrible day were 588. 1/6th had done only a little less badly. The CO, Lieutenant-Colonel W H Franklin, had been badly wounded and 22 other officers were killed or wounded, with 466 casualties for the whole battalion.

Of the four battalions of 93 Bde only 18/DLI, badly damaged as they were, had the ability to form a defence line, 400 yards behind the dead and wounded of the Leeds Pals who lay where they had been at 7.30 am. The two Bradford Pals battalions were equally wrecked. By 11 am the brigade's sector was quiet save for some desultory German shelling, but although the sound of battle had gone it was replaced by the heart rending cries of hundreds of wounded men. For those who were not too badly injured, attempts to crawl back to their line was likely to result in sudden death at the hands of alert German snipers. In the trenches themselves the survivors struggled to rebuild their defences against an anticipated German counter attack.

15/West Yorks, the Leeds Pals, had lost their CO wounded and out of action even before his men had gone over the top. His second in command, Stanley Neil, who had joined the Pals as a private, was killed along with nine other officers. 528 of their men were casualties.

The 1st Bradford Pals had lost their commander, Major C S Guyon, killed and had 515 casualties; the 2nd, who had never even got into No Man's Land, had 490 casualties and their CO, Lieutenant-Colonel M N Kennard, killed. With the exception of D Coy, 18/DLI had also failed to reach No Man's Land; at the time of their relief on the night of 4th/5th July they had lost 12 officers and 406 other ranks.

C Coy and three platoons of B Coy from 12/KOYLI, the Pioneer battalion, had gone into action with 93 Bde. They had worked like demons in supporting and succouring their battered comrades. They made endless, blood-soaked, journeys back and forth with dead and wounded; they had redug, shored up and cleared collapsed trenches and dugouts; they had buried remains of men in the bottom of trenches and all the while had to do this under a rain of death falling about them. At mid-morning, because the Pioneers were the only battalion resembling a coherent force, they were ordered to act as infantry in face of the expected German attack and took up defensive positions along the division's right boundary in Sackville Street.

On the left of the division the 94th Brigade were also back from where they had started – a shattered remnant. Some had made it into the German first and second line trenches, and a few glistening plates had been spotted on the western edge of the village, indicating that some had got that far. They simply faded away. In February 1917 a handful of Accringtons and Sheffield men were found buried, unidentifiable, in the village. Doubtless they were simply cleared away by the garrison along with the rest of the debris of battle.

The commander of 11/East Lancs, the Accrington Pals' Lieutenant-Colonel W Rickman had established his headquarters in C Sap, one of **Lt-Colonel** the five that had been dug out into No Man's Land. He found himself **Rickman** cut off from his brigade headquarters with all the telephone wires destroyed, despite the fact that they had been buried. Indeed they had been cut before the infantry battle had begun. His only means of communication was by runners, and few of these were to survive intact the 800 yards gap between the two headquarters. From his vantage point he had seen the waves of his men go past him, struggle up the slope towards the enemy line, many with their heads bent down as though walking into rain, and then they withered away as they fell victim to the German fire.

By midday the battle had, to all intents and purposes, ceased on this front. Lieutenant-Colonel Rickman gathered the survivors still behind the front line into some

The village of Serre and the main objective of 94 Brigade, which a handful of the attackers may have reached on the morning of 1st July, 1916. When the Germans withdrew the following year some unidentified bodies of Accrington and Sheffield men were found buried in Serre.

sort of defensive position on the eastern edge of the copse and with the help of the attached pioneers tried to move the hundreds of dead and wounded that lay about them. A few heroic stretcher bearers were moving about upright, the Germans permitted this mercy until some infantry began to fire at exposed Germans. Then all British troops in front of the German wire became targets.

The 1st Barnsley Pals (13/Y&L), whose task was to follow the Accringtons going for the centre of the village, had come down from the far side of the valley, across the ruined trenches whose bridges had all been blown away, and proceeded through the mud, shattered tree stumps and debris of Luke and Mark Copse, trying to get into No Man's Land. None of them managed to penetrate the German wire. Their task now was for those who remained to consolidate with the East Lancs survivors.

The Sheffield City Battalion faced a misfortune early on. Their CO, Lieutenant-Colonel Crosthwaite, the only professional officer in the battalion and who had been badly wounded at Ypres, collapsed and had to be evacuated; although a blow, it is almost certain that his presence would have made no difference to what took place subsequently. The 2 i/c, Major A Placket had his headquarters dugout in the middle of the shattered John Copse. He suffered the same fate of watching his battalion disintegrate, with only a very few men penetrating into the German second line. He soon became a casualty himself and was taken out of the line; it was left to a few young officers who were still on their feet (although all were wounded) to organise the survivors of Sheffield's pride, its City battalion.

The battalion on the extreme left of the whole British attack was 2nd Barnsley Pals (14/Y&L). In the front they only had two platoons, in position at the top, northern corner of John Copse, in Nairne Trench. Their task was to attack straight ahead and connect their trench to the captured German trenches so that there would be a new fire trench facing north, the beginnings of that 3,000 yard shield that was to be created by the division. The remainder of the battalion was in a series of trenches behind them on the western slope, with their commander, Lieutenant-Colonel Hulke, and his headquarters, in Roland Trench.

Like all the others, 2nd Barnsleys suffered casualties as it advanced at 7.30 am, in this case to follow on after the men from Sheffield. The CO decided at about 10 am that he would reinforce the two platoons whose job it was to create the new fire trench. 2/Lt Johnson was sent forward to Nairne Trench to help with the opening up of the Russian sap which had been dug by Barnsley miners into No Man's Land. (A

Russian sap was a shallow tunnel which could easily be broken open to the surface, and thereby creating an instant trench under cover.) When he came to the location he could find nothing – no Nairne Trench, no sap, no survivors of the two platoons. There had been complete annihilation on this the steepest incline on the division's front.

94 Brigade's casualties mirrored 93's. The Accrington Pals lost 585; Lieutenant-Colonel Rickman survived almost the whole of the first day, but was knocked out by a shell blast in the evening. He survived and returned to his battalion, which he was still commanding in the summer of 1918. The Official History seems to have lost sight of this; in its terse few pages on the action at Serre, a footnote comments on his death in action! The Sheffield City Battalion had gone into action with 680 men in the front line; they suffered 512 casualties. Both the Barnsley Pals battalions lost over 400 men, whilst the divisional pioneers, 12/KOYLI had lost 192 - men who were not there to fight with anything more offensive than a shovel had lost a third of their complement.

All thoughts of continuing the offensive against Serre had ended long before noon. The concern of the two brigadiers now lay in the intentions of the Germans, and the real possibility of a counter-attack. Although the British defences were in a perilous state, they were loath to bring forward the Hull brigade in the trenches behind them for fear that it would invite another massive German barrage, and the trench systems had been so hammered that there would be very little protection for 92 Brigade. In the end only a part of the Hull Commercials (10/East Yorks) were called forward to help the survivors and the pioneers reorganise and rebuild the divisional defences. The two companies sent forward, A and B, and 12/KOYLI did a magnificient job of clearing, repairing, rebuilding and supplying under trying conditions, ever fearful of a sniper's bullet.

The Germans did not attack; they had suffered damage themselves, they had defended their ground tenaciously and effectively, and in any case any attack across such shattered ground would have been difficult and possibly risky. They were content to reorganise themselves.

Brigadier-General Rees, commander of 94 Brigade.

As darkness fell brave men went out into No Man's Land to try and recover as many of the wounded and dead as possible; this went on every night until the division was relieved on the

A Clearing Station for the wounded on the Somme. *Opposite*: In the local newspapers the terrible tragedy gradually unfolded. The impact on communities, because of the Pals Battalions' recruiting method, was staggering.

short summer night of 4th July. The shattered survivors left the hell of their trenches before Serre and walked the miles back to Warnimont Wood whence they had set off with such high hopes the previous week, but which for many must have felt like a lifetime ago.

The Pals ideal had ended in tears and grief; the impact on cities, towns and villages of recruiting for individual battalions from such a narrow source of manpower made the already bad casualties have a disproportionate effect. It was probably true of these battalions that everyone in these places knew someone who was a casualty at Serre. Although some battalions would suffer worse casualties in later actions, none had the same impact as this first great battle in which the infantry units of 31st Division had been involved; battalions built up over almost two years had lost so much of their manpower that they lost their character. It did not stop them, however, from becoming in many cases excellent fighting units.

As it was, the failure of 31st Division had very little impact on the battle, for only one division, and that on the extreme right, had achieved its first day objectives. This had captured a large hill top village (Montauban) after crossing another open but very wide valley and getting into their objective after three hours of fighting. The crucial

HEROIC SONS OF YORKSHIRE.

HEAVY CASUALTIES IN BIG ADVANCE.

LEEDS "PALS" BATTALION LOSES MANY MEN.

OFFICER IN COMMAND AMONG THE KILLED.

In the fighting in the British offensive last week-end no battalion appears to have suffered more severely than the Leeds "Pals" Battalion. Many more casualties are announced to-day as having occurred on July 1, a date which will long be a fateful memory in Leeds. Yesterday we announced the death of Captain E. C. Whitaker and Lieut. S. Morris Bickersteth, who had been officers in the battalion since its formation. To-day to the list of killed has to be added the names of Captain S. T. A. Neil, Lieut. J. G. Vause, and Sec.-Lieut. T. Willey.

Capt. Stanley T. A. Neil, who was temporarily in command of the battalion, was the second son of Mr. J. W. Neil, assistant to Mr. Geo. A. Hart, sewerage engineer of the Leeds Corporation. He was 27 years of age and unmarried. A civil engineer by profession, he was, before the war, the resident engineer (under Mr. C. J. Henzell, waterworks engineer to the Leeds Corporation) at New Leighton Reservoir. He also took a large share of the responsibility for the design and erection of the new camp at Colsterdale. Capt. Neil joined the "Pals" as a ranker when the battalion was formed. He was immediately promoted lieutenant, and given his captaincy just before they left for Egypt last December. He came home on leave last month, returning to France on Saturday, June 3. While in Leeds he visited the homes of most of the Leeds "Pals" who had fallen or had been wounded.

CAPT. S. T. A. NEIL. (Killed.)   2nd-LIEUT. WILLEY. (Killed.)

Photos: Hoskins.

Second-Lieut. Willey is the elder son of Mr. Arthur Willey, solicitor, for whom much sympathy has been expressed in Leeds to-day. Mr. Willey has received sympathetic letters from Major Hartley, who now commands the battalion in succession to Capt. (temporary Major) Neil. Another officer of the battalion writes:— It has been a terrible business for our poor battalion. I have asked several men about poor Tom Willey, and they say he was magnificent. He was the hero of the battalion, both with officers and men. From the bottom of my heart I grieve for you. I cannot write more now. Vause, Whitaker, Bickersteth, Neil, and many more are gone."

The death of Lieut. Tom Willey will cause widespread regret. Only 19 years of age, he was an undoubted favourite wherever he went. Educated at Roscoes College, Harrogate, and at Harrow, he was articled to his father, and joined the "Pals" as a private, being given a commission six months later. At his weight he was the best boxer in the battalion.

Mr. F. W. Vause, of 32 Clarendon Road, Leeds and

West Yorkshires, who was killed last Saturday, was the elder son of Mr. S. Shann, of 19, Glover Street, off Camp Road, Leeds. After eight years at Leeds Grammar School, he won an open science exhibition to Christ Church, Oxford, and it was whilst there that he was given a commission. He had been twice wounded before being killed.

Second-Lieutenant R. E. Thorne Huddart (31), who was killed on June 30, was the youngest son of the late Rev. Dr. Huddart, of Kirklington, near Thirsk, and Second-Lieutenant Wilfrid Preston (25), of the Colne Valley Territorials, who died on Tuesday from wounds received in action, was a member of the firm of W. Preston and Company, woollen merchants, Huddersfield, of which his father is principal. Second-Lieutenant R. B. Holmes, of the King's Royal Rifles, who died of wounds on July 1, was a partner in the firm of J. R. Holmes and Sons, Bingley.

The death is also reported of Lieutenant Sydney Newlands, the elder son of the Rev. R. W. Newlands, pastor of the Providence Place Congregational Church, Cleckheaton. He was serving with the West Yorkshire Regiment. Another Cleckheaton casualty is that of Lieu-

Second Lieut. GRAY. (Wounded.)   Capt. J. L. HESELTON. (Wounded.)

tenant C. S. Hyde (23), the second son of the Rev. T. D. Hyde, who has been killed. Before the war he was on the staff of the Union of London and Smith's Bank, in Leeds.

A well-known Leeds officer who has been wounded is Major Arthur Frank Hess, of the 8th Battalion Leeds Rifles. He is 31 years of age, and has been in the Territorials nearly 15 years. The eldest son of the late Dr. Hess, of Filey, he is a director of Adolph Hess and Brother (Limited), of Leeds.

After having had many adventures since the outbreak of war, Lieutenant John Millican (24), West Riding Regiment, is reported killed. At the outbreak of war he was interned in Germany, where he had been employed as an interpreter. He escaped after seven days' captivity.

Second Lieutenant Francis Martello Gray, West Yorkshire Regiment, who has been wounded, is the third son of Mr W. Martello Gray, the well-known Bradford accountant. He was engaged in business with his father.

Captain J. L. Heselton, West Yorkshire Regiment, who was wounded in the head, is a son of Mr. R. T. Heselton, chartered accountant, of Bradford. He has travelled extensively throughout the world.

Lieutenant Frederick Robert Benson Jowitt, who was killed in action, was the only son of the late Mr. J. H. Jowitt and of Mrs. Rinah M. Jowitt, of New Zealand, and grandson of the late Mr. Robert Benson Jowitt, of Harehills, Leeds.

difference lay not in the quality of command or soldiers but in the availability of heavier calibre guns, many of which belonged to the adjacent French army. As John Terraine has often pointed out, this was an artillery war.

When 31st Division got back to Bus and the miserable huts in Warnimont Wood a final reckoning could be made; it had suffered 4,500 casualties. There are several rivals for the unsavoury title of bloodiest part of the battlefield of the Somme on 1st July. 156 battalions took part in the action on that day, of which thirty had casualties of more than 500. No less than five of these – 1/8th Warwicks, 15 and 16/West Yorks, 12/Y&L and 11/East Lancs – were at Serre. Five other battalions had casualties greater than 400. If not the bloodiest spot, more than enough blood was spilt there. Yet the division was not done with Serre; in October it returned to Warnimont Wood and it was close by when 3rd Division launched its attack on Serre on 13th November.

---

[1] The one exception to this procedure was the 18th Durham Light Infantry. For no good reason that can be identified, the City of Durham was never compensated for its expenditure in the raising of this battalion.

Chapter Six

THE WINTER BATTLE, 13th NOVEMBER 1916

In October the 3rd Division came south to take part in what was the final battle of the Somme in 1916. The summer of 1916 had been the wettest of the war and the whole of the ground in and above the valley of the Ancre was a morass, a process encouraged by the persistent artillery duelling that had been going on since June. In the battle area nearly all trace of greenery had disappeared whilst the already poor roads and tracks were in an appalling state.

The division went into billets – tents, wooden huts and remnants of buildings in the woods and villages around Bus-les-Artois, four miles to the west of Colincamps. Returning to the same spot was 31st Division, once more rebuilt and reorganised since the disaster of the first day of the great battle. The place was crammed with men, horses, mules, limbers, casualty stations, supply dumps and all the paraphernalia of war.

As the troops approached the front line at Serre the ground conditions deteriorated. Just moving about required great energy and it was inevitable that everyone would get covered in mud. The War Diary of 8/King's Own reported on 1st November that in Railway Hollow conditions got so bad that men were trapped for hours, awaiting dark

With the onset of the winter rains in November the ground on the Somme Battlefield became an enormous churned up morass.

to be physically dragged out. Movement above ground had to take place because the communication trenches were in such an awful state, severely damaged by shellfire for the most part, and the rain had turned them into running streams. It was the thankless task of the pioneers and working parties from the battalions to try and keep these systems usable.

In No Man's Land the barbed wire lay as thickly as before. Since 1st July there was the added, gruesome feature of decomposing bodies and skeletons draped over it. Since then they would have been shot repeatedly, whilst in No Man's Land other pathetic bundles marked the spot where other soldiers lay. The rats were one of the few living things to benefit from the battle of the Somme.

The German lines, too, had been battered out of recognition. What

Despite their better constructed trenches the Germans also began to suffer from the wet weather. Here German soldiers struggle along one of their communication trenches a few miles to the south of Serre.

had once appeared from the air as four deep rings of defences were now reduced, apparently, to a vast number of lip-to-lip shell holes. The Germans also suffered from the wet and the mud, but remained resolute in defence of their hilltop village stronghold, despite the gradual erosion of their positions that had taken place over the last four months, to their south.

The work to prepare for battle was enormous. 20/KRRC (King's Royal Rifle Corps), the divisional pioneers, used large numbers of men to repair the roads. Besides their own number they employed anything from 200 to 2,000 other men from the infantry every day in October and the early days of November to work at this vital task. In addition they erected new barbed wire defences along the 1,500 yards of the division's front line – this done at night because of the dangerously exposed position and frequently under trench mortar and machine gun fire.

The infantry battalions concentrated on the communications trenches. 2/Royal Scots used 800 men on the night of 9th November to dig a thousand yards of new trench into the battle area.

The third battle for Serre (and for the Ancre heights to the south) was planned for 25th October, with 3rd Division on the left of V Corps. On the division's left was VII Corps, whose right hand division, the 31st, had bitter knowledge of Serre. That Division's contribution to this battle would be confined to the reserve brigade on 1st July, 92 (Hull) Brigade. 3rd Division consisted of a mixture of Regular and Service battalions. 76 Brigade would attack on the left, 8 on the right and 9 Brigade would be in reserve.

As on 1st July, the bad weather, this time alternating between rain and hard frosts, influenced the date of the attack, which was postponed until the second week of November. If the weather had continued to be too poor for much longer, the attack would probably have never happened – Gough, the commander of the Fifth Army responsible for the attack, had warned Haig of that.

On 11th November the British bombardment opened with a barrage of great intensity which lasted forty-eight hours. Now the British had heavier guns, and the German defenders must have had a terrible time of it.

General Gough commander of Fifth Army.

During the night of the 12th the two divisions began to make their way into the trenches, some of the men having to struggle nine miles

In the wet conditions the lowest area of trenches became streams; the above trench is about four feet deep in water.

laden with a load of at least sixty pounds. Although much work had been done on the roads, for much of the way the soldiers would have had to walk in the neighbouring fields, as priority went to wheeled traffic. The communications trenches were in a particularly bad way. The north south trench along the valley bottom, Rob Roy, had become a stream and was so blocked that 2/Suffolks, 650 of them, had to move into their front line position in John Copse by going over the top. Fortunately the night was quiet and they managed to stumble up the slope without incident. A and C companies of 10/RWF had occupied the ground between Mark and Matthew Copse before dawn on 12th November and remained there all day until replaced by B and D companies at midnight. They did not go far, as they were going to take their part in the assault.

The four battalions of 9 Bde, some of whose companies had been holding the front line until the two attacking brigades came forward, now withdrew to the trenches beyond La Signy Farm and Touvent Farm ridge, where they would stay in reserve awaiting further orders as the progress of the battle dictated.

The pioneers, 20/KRRC, arrived in the area during the night of the 12th. B Company took up a position in the cellars of La Signy Farm from where they could see all that took place after zero hour. The remainder of the battalion went forward to Courcelles, D Company moving close to Euston Dump for the purpose of maintaining the light tramway in a working condition.

At 2 am on the 13th all was quiet, the shelling had not yet started. Then 2/Suffolks narrative of the operation reported a bell sounding across the battlefield, tolling a warning from the ruined church at Puisieux, to the north of Serre. Obviously the Germans knew of the impending attack.

The four battalions of 92 Brigade made their way forward, onto the open ground to the north of John Copse, led by 12th and 13/East Yorks who would attack up the slope on the left of 2/Suffolks. 10th and 11/East Yorks took up their place behind them on the slope in front of Hebuterne. These battalions all contained a high proportion of their original members, having avoided the carnage of 1st July. 93 Brigade, on their left, had only about thirty percent of its original members. It would not take part in this attack.

The very early hours of 13th November were frosty and clear; whilst waiting for zero hour at 5.30 am the infantry crouched in their trenches, some asleep on their haunches, as miners do.

At Serre this meant eight battalions of 3rd Division, 5,300 bayonets, and on their left 2,500 from 31st Division. Besides themselves, their rifles were covered in slimy and cloying mud, despite best endeavours to keep them clean; many would not be able to fire because of it. The men were also cold and wet through; tea laced with rum was issued to most of them between four and five.

By this stage the shelling on both sides had recommenced. At zero hour the barrage would lift a hundred yards and a similar distance every five minutes thereafter. The infantry would have to keep up if they were to ensure its vital protection. As before, much depended on the destruction of the German wire; in the four months since July the Germans had reinforced it with concertina wire which was even more difficult to destroy.

Shortly after 5 am the first platoons of all the five leading battalions climbed out of their trenches and went forward forty yards to lie down in a bed of mire. The battalions were to advance in eight closely packed waves, their objective Serre.

At this stage a thick fog descended. Fog is a double-edged weapon; it causes confusion and disorientation amongst the attackers; but also masks them from machine gunners and enemy artillery. With the dawn came a light drizzle. Visibility was reduced to a few yards. Meanwhile artillery fire on both sides was building up to a crescendo, with

Moving up to the attack along a newly dug trench.

numerous casualties amongst the three brigades. The atrocious condition of the trenches became worse and many of the wooden bridges across them, to make possible the speedy movement of support battalions, destroyed. A planned smoke screen on 3rd Division front was abandoned, but smoke candles were lit on the left flank of 92 Brigade. The weather made artillery observation utterly impractical, whilst aircraft observation was impossible. The two tanks allocated to the left flank could not be used because even here the going would be too heavy and they would have been bogged down.

The German artillery barrage came down from 3.30 am, searching the whole battle area. At Serre the attacking troops were not as lucky as those further south. For here the advances along Thiepval Ridge during the course of the battle meant that the British artillery could attack the German defences in enfilade. It was too far to be able to do this at Serre, and indeed the German artillery to the north could catch the advancing British in enfilade. The balance was fine between another disaster and success.

8/East Yorks had the furthest to go. They were in the same position as 18/DLI on 1st July and at zero hour they moved forward from their positions between Flag and Southern Trenches. They had to cross a thousand yards of broken bridges, shattered trenches and shell torn ground before they reached the front and on to support 2/Royal Scots. As they filed slowly forward the German barrage caught D Company, which was bringing up the rear. This caused many casualties within minutes of their move from the relative safety of their trenches. At about 7 am the first two waves found the gaps in the wire that B Company had found earlier and went through the German first line. They proceeded across the second line until they were stopped and mixed with the Scots in the same desperate search for cover from the murderous fire. By 7.30 am the last two waves had reached the German front line but found that further movement was impossible.

As had been the case on the left, Germans emerged from behind their attackers from their deep underground shelter. It was almost impossible to tell friend from foe; with the loss of officers, poor visibility, enemies seemingly on every side, and confronted by uncut wire, many troops who had gone before the East Yorks and were now leaderless and disorientated started to withdraw in a disorganised way and stumbled back to their own trenches. Despite the efforts of the officers of the East Yorks to halt this, they found themselves being swept back as if before a crowd.

Once again the Brigadiers were faced with the dilemma which had taxed Ingles and Rees on 1st July. By 9 am, as the fog cleared, it was clearly obvious from their vantage point that most of the attack of 3rd Division had failed. Yet one battalion alone, 10/RWF, directly in front of 76 Brigade, was so near to success and had done all that had been asked of it and were still holding their gains at the German fourth line. They also knew that 13/East Yorks of 31st Division's 92 Brigade were in possession of the German third line. The enemy shelling was spelling disaster, however, falling on the thousands of men floundering about in the quagmire and trapped in many places by uncut wire. The question was whether or not to commit 9 Brigade to the attack. Would it carry the day or would it so weaken the position if they failed that the Germans could advance into the British lines in a counter attack?

All had not gone the enemy's way. At least 450 of them had been captured; the RWF alone captured a hundred in front of Mark Copse. Many of the prisoners were to be killed by their own bombardment.

At 10 am the Brigadiers decided to order part of the reserve battalions to form a defensive line at the bottom of the valley between Campion, Mark and Rob Roy. Half of 13/King's Own was sent into 76 Brigade's sector and one company each from 4/RF and 12 West Yorks went to 8 Brigade on the right. Obviously the attack had failed and Serre had defied the British for a second time.

The battle continued to develop. On the left 13/East Yorks came under fire from their own artillery. It is another classic example of how vital communications are in battle; for the Gunners did not know how far they had penetrated and they recommenced their shelling of Serre. Indeed even the Divisional commander, Major General Deverell, had his direct communications with the two divisions on either side of him cut at 10 am, and they were not restored until 4.30 pm. Besides being shelled by their own side, 13/East Yorks faced a threat from Germans behind them who had emerged from their underground shelters, passed over by the advancing British in the general confusion and murk. 12/East Yorks were still some way behind and could not get through to them because of the German shelling and the newly emerged enemy. It was at this time that the only Victoria Cross awarded in all the fighting for Serre was won.

'No 12/21, John Cunningham, Private, 12th Bn East Yorkshire Regt. For most conspicuous bravery and resource during operations. After the enemy's front line had been captured, Private Cunningham proceeded with a bombing section up a communication trench. Much opposition was encountered, and the rest of the section became casualties. Collecting all the bombs from the casualties, this gallant soldier went on alone. Having expended all his bombs, he returned for a fresh supply, and again proceeded to the communication trench, where he met a party of ten of the enemy. These he killed, and cleared the trench up to the enemy line. His conduct throughout the day was magnificent.'

London Gazette, 13 Jan 1917.

He was the first Hull man to win the VC. He survived the war and died in Hull in 1941 at the age of 43.

The problems of 13/East Yorks continued. D Company had got further forward than any other company, but now found itself surrounded. Their commander, Captain Wooley, decided that he and his surviving eight men would have to surrender when a large body of Germans were seen approaching his right flank with a number of British soldiers in front of them. He had no wish to fire on the captured British and at 3.30 pm his men joined the other forty from the battalion as prisoners of war.

10th and 11/East Yorks had not been put into the fight with the exception of two Lewis guns and twelve men from the 10th. They were posted at the extreme left of the 12th and had succeeded in stopping a drive to cut it off, killing sixty or so but at the cost of ten of their own

Map 9. The British Trench System before Serre 1916

N

who were killed, wounded or missing.

At 5 pm the attack by 92 Brigade was finished and 12th and 13/East Yorks were withdrawn, struggling back in the dusk to their own trenches. The day for the Hull men, their second time in battle at Serre, had been a bitter one. 12/East Yorks had set out with eighteen officers; only two returned unwounded, eight had been killed and the total casualties of officers and men were 385. 13/East Yorks had lost seven officers killed and four captured with a total casualty list of 430. The other two battalions who had remained in reserve throughout suffered 97 casualties, largely a result of the German shelling.

On 92 Brigade's right, the divisional pioneers, (20/KRRC) had a very busy day. Their most urgent task was the maintenance of the light railway which ran out of Railway Hollow in a south westerly direction, skirting Basin Wood on its way to Euston Dump and the RAMC Dressing Station just beyond. It was an essential requirement for this battle, it would usually take four men to carry a stretcher laden with a man, but the deep mud made this carrying task almost impossible and in any case the limited number of stretcher bearers would have been overwhelmed by the numbers that required their services. The German bombardment could hardly avoid missing it, and it tore gaps in the line and hit trains and their wagons. A platoon of D Company under Lieutenant Penna, working in the battle zone, spent almost the whole day in the open but miraculously avoided being blown to bits. They relaid line time after time as sections were blown apart. The fatalities would doubtless have been far greater if this essential service for the wounded had not been carried out.

20/KRRC remained in the sector for a further three months, through the dreadful winter of 1916 and early 1917. They supervised or redug themselves the communication trenches and lay drains to take the deep streams out of the front line and Rob Roy trenches. On 20th November it set about establishing a formidable barrier of barbed wire to protect the British lines before the full onset of winter. Their work continued night after night until they had built an impressive obstacle almost a mile in length which was given the name the Yellow Line.

In the front-line fighting on 13th November, on the left of 76 Brigade, 2/Suffolks had a very trying day. Their advance had quickly petered out in front of the German wire, yet it was essential for the survival of 13/East Yorks on their left and 10/RWF on their right that the battalion keep up to schedule. Their failure to do so left these battalions exposed and in danger of being cut off. By 6.30 am, only forty five minutes after their start, six of the seven officers of C and D

Written on the back of this photograph is the following: '*A wonderfully clear picture of the actual ground we had to traverse on Nov. 13/1916 at Serre, shewing double belts of extra heavy enemy wire and shocking mud and water, which explains why several men were drowned in the attack.*'

Companies on the right had fallen and most of the battalion had come to a halt in No Man's Land. At 7 am what remained of the Suffolks had managed to get back to their own trenches in John Copse; battalion headquarters was then moved six hundred yards back, across the valley, into Monk Trench. As a fighting force the battalion was finished and now all that the survivors could do was to prepare themselves for a highly probable counter-attack. By nightfall casualties were eleven officers and 522 men, of whom certainly a number, probably about forty, had become prisoners – a casualty total as awful as that of the Sheffield City Battalion on 1st July.

8/King's Own had followed the Suffolks but soon found their forward movement blocked by German fire and the hundreds of

Suffolks occupying the trenches and shell holes which they had intended to use. At 10 am C Company was withdrawn and combined with D Company in Rob Roy Trench; at least this freed up the trenches in the front line which were easy pickings for the German artillery. A Company withdrew from the position it had taken in the German front line in the evening, and with the rest of the battalion retired to Campion Trench to take up a defensive position. Roll call at first light showed the battalion's casualties to be 103.

On the right of 76 Brigade 10/RWF had done very well, showing how near success had been for 3rd Division – well cut wire would have made all of the difference. Despite their unprotected flanks, because of the failure of the Suffolks and the two Scottish battalions to take ground, they had reached the top of the valley and were some only dozens of yards from a pile of bricks that had been a farm in the village.

In their advance they had taken numerous German prisoners, adding to the confusion in Matthew Copse where they were despatched. Because of the vulnerability on each side, half companies had to form defensive flanks and this reduced the impetus forward. At 8.30 am the advance stopped before the Germans' fourth line. Many defenders now emerged from their deep shelters beneath the village and swamped Captain Rudd and the survivors of B Company who simply disappeared from view. The Welshmen now consolidated in the third line, knee deep in mud, alongside a small group of 1/Gordons who had been able to fight through to them. From this position they withdrew in an orderly fashion by stages until, at 7 pm, in darkness, the last few returned behind the British wire into the remnants of Copse Trench. 10/RWF had lost seven of their nineteen officers killed and had a total of 297 casualties.

1/Gordons had suffered 141 casualties at the end of the day. Their last men came back to the trenches with the Welsh and then made their way to the rest of the battalion in Monk and Dunmow trenches.

8 Brigade had a terrible day as well, and for all its exertions got nowhere. 1/RSF, who had tried to shelter the Welsh right flank had been unable to progress beyond the uncut wire of the German second line. The barrage had been relatively ineffectual here and by 7.15 am the Fusiliers were driven back by the weight of the German shelling and rifle fire. The survivors, disorganised and out of touch because of the fog, returned to their own line in the open ground on the division's right flank. They had suffered 205 casualties.

The regulars of 2/Royal Scots suffered even worse than their fellow

Scots. Around 8 am the German bombardment was particularly heavy, falling on the battalion out in the open in front of their own wire and crowded together due to the uncut wire which had held up the leading companies. Men started to struggle back down the valley's eastern slope, mixing with the Light Infantrymen and East Yorks who were following their battalion.

A party of one hundred men from various battalions were organised by Captain Strange and Lieutenant Scott and put to work firing from the British front line and the many shell holes in front of it. It was a common complaint that the men were beginning to forget how to use their rifles at about this stage of the war, and the rifle fire that these men provided, aimed at enemy machine gun posts and whatever of the Germans they could see did valuable service. This was maintained for most of the day until they were relieved by two companies of 12/ West Yorks brought forward from 9 Brigade. 2/Royal Scots suffered 270 casualties, including Captain Spofford who had managed to lead B Company into the German second line.

7/KSLI had made very little progress and remained for most of the day at the German front line. Their casualties were heavy along their 400 yards of front; in the late afternoon they reformed in the area of Dunmow and Flag trenches, utterly exhausted and with 216 casualties.

The last of the attacking battalions, 8/East Yorks, crossed almost a thousand yards of shell-swept ground with some men getting as far as the German line, where they were halted, though most of the battalion was well behind them. These few were unable to hold on to the ground which they had gained and by 10 am the majority were back behind the British wire where the officers tried to reorganise a defensive line, further attacks being out of the question. They remained there the whole day in trenches which had become nothing much more than water filled ditches. The battalion suffered 236 casualties.

When night fell the whole division was in the trenches from where it had started.

In the area of 76 and 8 Brigades in the valley the eight battered battalions were reinforced with elements of 13/King's Own, 12/West Yorks and 4/RF, for a German counter-attack, although most unlikely, had not been ruled out. Only 1/NF remained in reserve, in the trenches close to the ruined track from Euston Dump to Hebuterne, but at 11 am they also moved forward to the Great Northern Avenue, from where they could see the battlefield.

In the one day his division had suffered more than two thousand casualties, to which had to be added the over 800 of 92 Brigade of 31st

Division. Serre had exacted another awful toll. The three attacks – that of the French in June 1915, and of the British on 1st July and 13th November 1916 had resulted in almost twenty thousand killed, wounded and missing amongst the attackers on those days.

The reason for 3rd Division's failure, when it came close to success, again lies with the artillery. It had failed to cut the German wire – or rather, not enough of it. The mud had not helped in the task of cutting the wire, serving to help minimize effect of the shells. The fact that the Germans could also use their own artillery, from the north, in enfilade, made the British task that much more difficult. Uncut wire was the crucial factor contributing to the failure of the British.

The mud was a major impediment for the attackers. The fog probably had a broadly neutral effect – it prevented artillery observation and caused dislocation amongst the advancing British. On the other hand it also meant that the German machine gunners were often firing blind as well, and may well have contributed to a less bloody result for the British.

The Battle of the Somme came to an end on 18th November; there were further attacks to the south of Serre, on Redan Ridge and along the valley of the Ancre, working on British successes there on 13th November, but it was decided against renewing the attack on Serre. 3rd Division remained in front of Serre until 15th January 1917. The next attack would be made on Serre in July 1918; for in February 1917 the Germans withdrew from the awkward line that had been created by the Somme and secretly retired to their well prepared fortifications to the east, the Hindenburg Line.

Chapter Seven

THE GERMAN WITHDRAWAL – FEBRUARY 1917

On 24th February 1917 patrols from the Fifth Army reported that the Germans had pulled back from their front line trenches. 'Operation Alberich' (the deceitful dwarf of the Niebelung legend) was the German code word for a withdrawal to carefully prepared positions which they had named *Siegfried Stellung* – known as the Hindenburg Line by the British.

The secretive withdrawal straightened out a considerable bulge in the German front, and in the Serre front the depth of ground given up amounted to around twelve miles. Cautiously, the British and French troops pushed across the deserted positions and into countryside no longer pitted by shelling. What they did come across was a systematic devastation and spoiling: roads were mined, bridges broken, trees cut down, buildings that might provide shelter for troops had been burnt,

Map 10

water poisoned and booby traps set.

At last British soldiers were in the village of Serre and among them men of the 31st 'Pals' Division, though it was hardly a Pals Division any longer, replacements to the battalions had altered the parochial compostion. Among the men picking their way through the ruins of the village and surrounding old German trench systems was Private Tommy Oughton, ex 13th Battalion York and Lancs (1st Barnsley Pals). Tommy had developed dysentry in August 1916 and had been sent home to recuperate, but now he was back where he first saw action on the first day of the Battle of the Somme, this time though he had been posted to the sister battalion, the 2nd Barnsleys.

Tommy Oughton

'When I went back to the 14th we were going round the back of the Serre area. It was the time when Jerry was retiring, because we went up and followed through Serre. I remember I went down into their dug-outs, had a look round and examined them. They were grand places – they were deeper and as comfortable again as ours.'

For the unwary a dugout recently abandoned by the Germans was a dangerous place, for they showed great ingenuity in constructing all manner of killing and maiming traps. Lumps of coal were left with detonators hidden inside. A piece of timber, part of the cladding on the dugout wall, might be sticking out with its nail in place waiting for an unsuspecting Tommy to effect a repair – the nail point was lined up on a detonator which in turn fired an explosive charge. An attractive

At last the German defences at Serre are in British hands – spring 1917.

Atmospheric image of war. This was taken on the road leading into Serre from the direction of Mailly-Maillet in 1917.

souvenir such as a Luger pistol or binoculars could be wired to explosives. A shovel might be stuck between timbers in a dugout waiting for someone to retrieve it; upon its removal a charge was fired.

Added to this the Germans fought a rear-guard action as they withdrew and shelled areas when they knew that the Tommies were moving in. Up the road from Serre, less than a mile from the village on the Puisieux Road, on 9th March, RSM Polden was scouting ahead of elements of the 12th York and Lancs (Sheffield City Battalion) when heavy shelling started. Men and horses of other units were caught in the barrage and many were killed and wounded. RSM Polden organised the remaining men and aided the wounded 'setting' – as his citation for the Military Cross says – 'a fine example of conduct under fire'.

Now that the old Somme battlefields of 1916 were behind the British lines the gruesome task of clearing up the remains of those who had fallen in the fighting for the German stronghold could begin. Cemeteries began to be established and one Sheffield City man, Lance Corporal Reg Glenn, recalled the occasion:

'The Padre asked me if I would accompany him to visit our

91

With the German withdrawal No Man's Land revealed its grim harvest of slain dating from 1st July, 1916. No longer 'missing in action' the remains could be identified and given a decent burial.

old front line and No Man's Land, which was littered with British dead. Ours were in lines where they had fallen. They were just skeletons in khaki rags and their equipment. We walked up to the old German wire – the Padre had brought a friend with him – and the three of us turned back to look towards our lines. Then the Padre said a prayer for the dead and we sang the Hymn, 'For All the Saints'. Next morning the dead were buried by an overnight fall of snow. It was some weeks before No Man's Land was cleared when V Corps began to make new cemeteries to finally lay our pals to rest.'

Written on the back of this photograph is the following: *'The appalling destruction of Serre village, which we attacked on 13/11/1916, shewing also Serre Wood remains, our immediate objective.'*

Other Pals battalion members sought out their 1st July 1916 'missing' among the debris of war so that they could be given a decent burial. The Yorkshire cricketer Lieutenant Booth, of the Leeds Pals, was identified by his cigarette case which had been a gift from the MCC when he took part in a tour of South Africa. Leeds Pals soldier Private Arthur Pearson recalled the grim task which took place in the early spring of 1917:

'Months afterwards when he [the Germans] had abandoned Serre, a party of 'Old Boys' were sent up to the old sector we had attacked over and we identified several bodies. One was our Company Commander [Captain Whitaker]. We put what was left of him into a sandbag and carried him down to a cemetery. We had the Padre with us and he read the burial service as we buried him.'

Thus ended an episode concerning the fighting around the village of Serre. However, the killing fields around this cluster of wrecked houses had not finished reaping lives – the Germans would be back.

The written caption on the back of this photograph reads: *'All that is visible to-day of the famous Serre Wood in front of Serre village attacked by us on Nov. 13/1916. This gives a good idea of the weird results of H.E. shells hitting large trees'.*
Below: The road into Serre from Puisieux at 'Flank Trench', 1917.

A working party at Serre in 1917.
Below: Puisieux in 1917. Looking down the road to Bucquoy from crossroads of Serre-Miraumount Road. (D919/D6)

Puisieux 1917. Looking north towards Essarts.
Below: Broad gauge railway being laid round Puisieux. Line passed in front of 'John', 'Luke' and 'John' copses. The bed of this line is still discernible today and some its sleepers have been used occasionally as fence posts.

Chapter Eight

THE FINAL BATTLE, SUMMER 1918

The collapse of Russia and its transformation during 1917-1918 into the Soviet Union had provided the Germans with an opportunity to transfer huge resources from the Eastern Front, where most of their aggressive actions had taken place after the failure of the Schlieffen Plan, to the Western Front. Their aim was to strike a decisive blow before the arrival en masse of United States troops should push the military balance decisively in favour of the Entente powers. It is worth dwelling on the extraordinarily harsh terms that the Germans imposed upon the defeated Russians; what might a German military victory have imposed on Britain, France and Italy?

The German offensive planned for the spring of 1918 called for a massive concentration of troops, numbers of them specially trained storm troops, and artillery. They were to launch an attack on the link between the French and British armies, which meant against the weak Fifth Army, which lay astride the Somme, commanded by Gough. Their intentions were reasonably clear to their opponents, and indeed a defence scheme which laid much less emphasis on holding continuous lines of trenches and was not averse to losing chunks of ground, temporarily it was hoped, if need be, was in place. But this was a period of some disorder, both politically and militarily, for the French and the British. The French had suffered a series of mutinies in their army, the extent of which seems, amazingly, to have escaped the Germans. It was not an offensive force for quite some time, especially under the cautious Pétain, whose energies were concentrated on rebuilding its strength and morale. The British had undergone a great slog at Third Ypres, better known as Paschendaele, had enjoyed a brief moment of triumph at Cambrai in November 1917, only to have it dashed, and had sent valuable divisions to Italy at the end of that year to shore up Italy's crumbling defences. On top of this the BEF underwent a fundamental reorganisation of divisions in February 1918; this reduced the number of infantry battalions from four in a brigade to three, giving an infantry division of nine battalions instead of twelve. There had been considerable disagreement about how to deal with the manpower shortage, which can be studied elsewhere. Haig's favoured option was to retain the size of divisions, but to reduce their number.

German storm troopers begin their attack 21st March, 1918. Soon the old Somme battlefields would once again be in their hands – including the village of Serre.

He considered that the weak area lay in finding enough adequately trained and experienced staff officers to maintain the number of divisions that existed. He was overruled and the result was, often, a quite chaotic disbanding of battalions, amalgamations and transferrals to completely new formations, with all the impact that had on the efficiency of formations.

The Germans launched their attack on 21st March. By 25th March they had overrun Bapaume and on the 26th they had crossed the Ancre, captured Serre and had advance parties in Hebuterne and Colincamps. On that same day at a meeting in Doullens, to the west of Arras, Foch was appointed as the Supremo of the allied forces.

At the same time that Foch was appointed, General Byng, commanding the Third Army, was given allied command of all forces

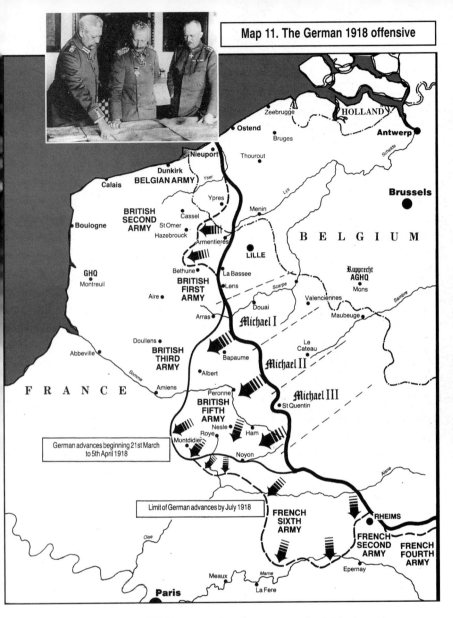

Map 11. The German 1918 offensive

north of the Somme. IV Corps, under the command of Lieutenant-General Sir G M Harper, was in the area of Hebuterne, and it was into this formation that the New Zealand Division, assembling west of Amiens, was sent piecemeal. It arrived in any available transport to Ribemont, but many of the troops had to march. By dawn of 26th March some of the division had arrived at Mailly Maillet; by mid-

British troops fighting to stem the German advance which threatened to drive through to the Channel in the spring of 1918. The old Somme positions were recaptured and once more the Germans were back again in the ruins of the village of Serre.

morning they were in action against the German advance troops at the Sucrerie, on the crossroads before Colincamps.

Australian troops were sent forward to join 62nd Division with orders to recover Hebuterne on IV Corps' left flank. The New Zealanders did not reach full strength until 28th March and the German progress in this sector was stabilised. The German advance was suffering from exhausted troops, over-extended lines of communication and supply over the desert which the battle areas of the previous years had become and stiffening resistance from the defenders.

The Germans were holding a very similar position to that of June 1915 before the French offensive. Hebuterne was still held by the British and the Germans held the blood-soaked battlefields of 1915 and

1916. The Germans had made huge and impressive gains in ground, but it was quite clear that the strategic objective had failed, and Ludendorff switched his interest to the Ypres Salient and the Lys.

On 7th June the New Zealand Division was relieved by 42nd (East Lancs) Division, which had been engaged in fighting the German advance three miles to the north, on the Bapaume-Arras road, withdrawing eventually to Bucquoy. The New Zealand Division did not return to the line until the first week of July, this time to the north of Serre, facing Puisieux. On 26th July they suffered the loss of the most renowned fighting man in the division, Sergeant R C Travis of the 2nd Otago Regt. Dubbed the 'King of No Man's Land', he was the holder of the DCM and MM when he was killed at Rossignol Wood and posthumously awarded the Victoria Cross.

42nd Division had the proud honour of being the first Territorial Force division to be sent abroad for active service when it was sent to Egypt in September 1914. It campaigned at Gallipoli and in Egypt, but was ordered to France in February 1917. It fought before the Hindenburg Line and in Third Ypres, Nieuport and in the relatively quiet, flat zone east of Bethune. On 15th October 1917 it came under **Sergeant** the command of Major-General A Solly-Flood who had begun his war **R C Travis** as a major fighting at Mons. He developed a reputation as a first rate communicator and trainer of men; he coined the division's motto, 'Go one better'.

The 42nd moved from the area of Hannescamps, Essarts and Bienvillers au Bois to be quartered in the same villages and woods around Bus-les-Artois and Bertrancourt that had housed 3rd and 31st divisions in their battles for Serre. The men of 1/5th East Lancs had particularly close links with the Accrington Pals. They had a front of 3,800 yards facing the Germans across the Hebuterne-Colincamps Plain. They immediately began a campaign of probes and attacks in company strength on the enemy's outposts and front line, close to the track connecting the two villages.

The great offensive of the allies was to commence in August; the intervening period was used to establish superiority locally and to train new recruits in the realities of war with these small scale, but effective, operations. The British line gradually inched forward. The Germans made great use in these weeks of poison gas using their long range guns in the valley behind Pys. This made life hazardous for man and horse alike, particularly for the infantry and for the divisional artillery concentrated in front of Sailly au Bois.

By the end of July, 127 (Manchester) Brigade had taken La Signy

Farm, and could look down on the 1916 battlefield, also forcing the enemy to withdraw from Staff Copse, 500 yards west of Toutvent Farm. The Germans still occupied the 1916 brigade headquarters in Observation Wood. Alongside 42nd Division, the New Zealanders, joined by a battalion of Americans from 137th Regiment, carried on similar probing attacks against the defenders of Puisieux.

On 10th August Lance Sergeant Edward Smith of 1/5th Lancashire Fusiliers, with a small number of men, raided Touvent Farm only to find it empty. He suspected that the deep trenches would be reoccupied at night from across the valley, and therefore determined to ambush them. His patrol remained in occupation of the farm.

Just before dusk, as expected, a large number of men were seen to approach up the slope from Railway Hollow. He engaged them with Lewis gun and rifle fire and caused casualties amongst the unsuspecting Germans; he then skilfully withdrew his men back to their own lines, west of Staff Copse, without loss. He was awarded the DCM for this exploit. Most divisions had men of outstanding accomplishments and Edward Smith was one of these. Twelve days later, after the division had gone through Serre, he won the Victoria Cross, storming a German machine gun post at the Lozenge. He

Lance Sergeant Edward Smith

survived the war to return to France, still with the Lancashire Fusiliers, in 1939 as a Lieutenant (Quartermaster's Commission). He died in January 1940 and is buried in Beuvry Communal Cemetery Extension – his battalion having served, ironically enough, at Beuvry in February 1918.

On the night of 12th - 13th August the Germans made three separate assaults on the British line. At this time it was held by 127 Brigade, occupying the remnants of the 1916 trenches in Mark, Luke and John Copses. It was to be their last attack in this area. The Germans now began to withdraw their battered troops from this line, suffering also a steady infiltration by the New Zealand Division to the north, between Serre and Puisieux. The Germans finally gave up their hold on Serre on the evening of 19th August and 42nd Division passed through it and took up position for Third Army's part in the Advance to Victory. They moved across a village filled with damaged guns, transport, dead men and horses, strewn with unexploded projectiles, cartridge cases and masses of rusty barbed wire.

The Fourth Battle, more like a siege, had lasted ten weeks for 42nd Division and had cost them less than a thousand casualties. Although only a footnote, perhaps, in the light of the great things going on around them, Serre had finally fallen to British arms.

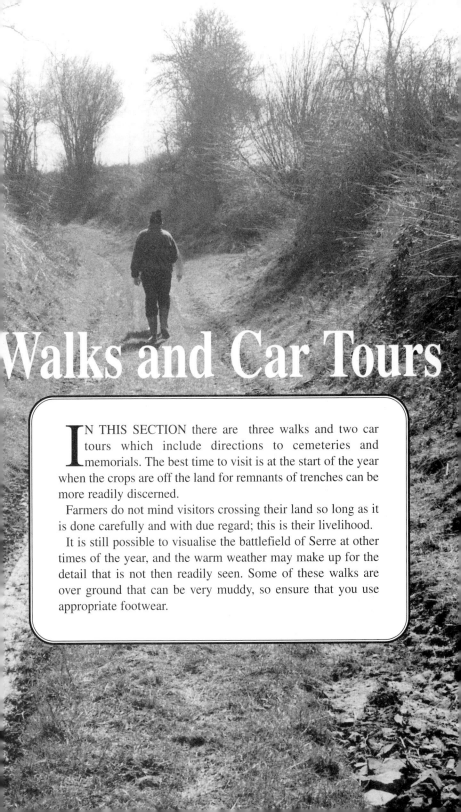

Walks and Car Tours

IN THIS SECTION there are three walks and two car tours which include directions to cemeteries and memorials. The best time to visit is at the start of the year when the crops are off the land for remnants of trenches can be more readily discerned.

Farmers do not mind visitors crossing their land so long as it is done carefully and with due regard; this is their livelihood.

It is still possible to visualise the battlefield of Serre at other times of the year, and the warm weather may make up for the detail that is not then readily seen. Some of these walks are over ground that can be very muddy, so ensure that you use appropriate footwear.

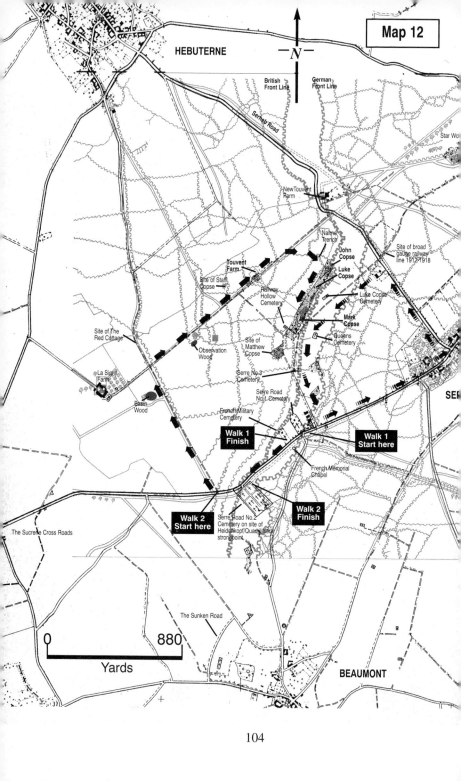

Map 12

HEBUTERNE

N

British Front Line

German Front Line

Serneb Road

Star Wo

New Touvent Farm

Site of broad gauge railway line 1917-1918

Nairne Trench

John Copse

Luke Copse

Touvent Farm

Site of Staff Copse

Railway Hollow Cemetery

Luke Copse Cemetery

Mark Copse

Queens Cemetery

Site of Matthew Copse

Site of The Red Cottage

Observation Wood

La Signy Farm

Basin Wood

Serre No 3 Cemetery

Serre Road No 1 Cemetery

French Military Cemetery

SE

Walk 1 Finish

Walk 1 Start here

French Memorial Chapel

Walk 2 Start here

Serre Road No 2 Cemetery on site of Heidenkopf/Quadrilateral stronghold

Walk 2 Finish

The Sucrerie Cross Roads

0   880

Yards

The Sunken Road

BEAUMONT

104

WALK 1.   Serre: The Battle Arena

Park beside Serre Road No 1 Cemetery.

Set off from here keeping to the left hand side of the road. Almost as soon as you start you are crossing the site of the German barbed wire and entering the defences of Serre. The small village is ahead of you; hardly any bigger than it was in the war. The first farm on the left was not there during the years of fighting, nor was the track beyond it with its signpost to various cemeteries. This was laid down to give the War Graves Commission access to these isolated cemeteries. Continue towards the village and look to the right - notice the trees running along the low ridge about 200 yards away. This was known as Ten Tree Alley. Looking beyond the village, behind it and to the right, and Pendant Copse, a domed shape wood, may be seen. It was there that those indomitable few of 18/DLI disappeared for ever after their heroic penetration of the German defences on 1st July.

The Serre battlefield is off to the left. On the right you should notice a calvary or crucifix, which is the start of Munich Trench (one of the longest trenches on the Somme). About a mile down that metalled track, on the left, you should see a Cross of Sacrifice which is part of Ten Tree Alley Cemetery, a place that is rarely visited.

Serre (and Puisieux) were adopted by Sheffield after the war and soon after you pass the village signpost you will see the memorial to their City Battalion

View of the battlefield from the south west looking towards Puisieux.

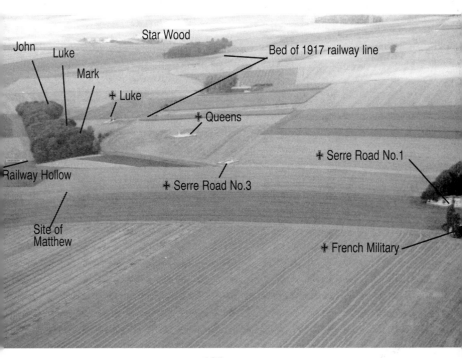

(12/Y&L) on the left. The ground, especially on the left, shows evident signs of digging, trenches, German defences and shell holes. At the time of writing a British 9" shell was being used as a gate stop for a house on the other side of the road.

Continuing to walk through the village, there is a narrow road on the left; this is Serheb Road, which goes to Hebuterne – **turn left** along it. It crosses the 1915 battle line of the French and that of 12 and 13/East Yorks in November 1916. The German defences can be quite easily distinguished in the fields that lie on either side of the road. Off to the right is where Capt Wooley of 13/East Yorks held out all day of 13th November until surrounded and captured. Also on the right, some 300 yards into the field and amongst the stunted trees, is the place where Pte Jack Cunningham won his VC.

Proceed until you come to a small modern house, set back from the road, on your left. There is a clear view over the open fields to Hebuterne. Just before reaching this there used to be two small British battlefield cemeteries. John Copse 1 and 2, which have long since been removed to Euston Road Cemetery. The farm in the dip in the valley on your quarter right was not there in 1914; it is new Touvent Farm and marks the approximate site where Roland Leighton was mortally wounded. The old one could not be rebuilt because the ground below it had been carved out as an underground fortress and barracks, complete with tunnels. Up the slope on the right came the two battalions of East Yorks through the deep mud of November 1916. Just beyond the house a track crosses the road which is the bed of the 1917 broad gauge railway line built by the British from Puisieux to Colincamps and beyond.

Turn left along it and proceed towards the woods on your right. The track goes through No Man's Land, and as the woods come closer the ground falls more sharply on the right towards Railway Hollow. The first of these woods was John Copse, and close to its northern edge and the incline is where Nairne Trench was, the grave of so many Barnsley men of 14/Y&L. On 1st July the trench was obliterated by artillery and with it two of their platoons. This was the planned pivot point of 31st Division and the most northerly tip of the attack on 1st July.

Remnants of the old railway line are to be found, particularly sleepers, some of which have been turned to good service as part of the posting for the fences. Usually there are shells and other battlefield debris by the side of the track awaiting collection by the bomb disposal teams that regularly tour the old battlefield.

On the right is Luke Copse British Cemetery, and a hundred yards to the right rear of it is the forward edge of John Copse. A ferocious bombardment fell on this part of the wood on the morning of 18th June, one shell of which buried CSM Marsden, whose body was never recovered. Jack Horsfall was in the wood early on a June morning two years or so ago, entirely alone. After a short time he was overcome by an overwhelming feeling of dread and he could not get out of the trees fast enough. This is not a particularly unusual sensation for a battlefield visitor. I had a similar experience when visiting Mort Homme near Verdun.

Luke Copse Cemetery is a long and narrow cemetery placed in front of Luke and John Copse, beyond the British barbed wire barricade and in the No Man's

106

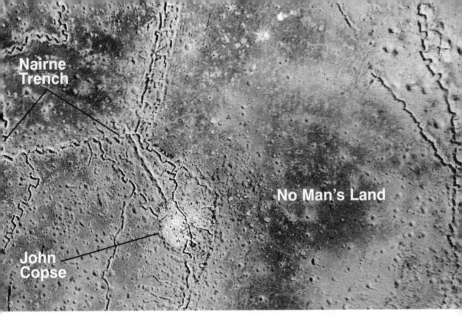

John Copse on morning of 1st July 1916

Land of the two 1916 battles. It was here, coming out of what is now a long, thin wood that the Sheffield City men came followed by 2/Barnsley Pals on 1st July and later, in the thick fog of 13th November, so did 2/Suffolks and 8/King's Own. This is one of a number of cemeteries created after the German withdrawal to the Hindenburg Line by V Corps Burial Officer. 38 out of the 72 burials are unknown. All of them had been lying on the battlefield for some months. Private J R Carding-Wells had come from Switzerland to enlist in September 1914; he was 19 when he died. The Gunstone brothers, also of the City battalion, enlisted on the same day and were killed on the same day. They were 24 and 25. Close to here was killed Corporal Alexander Robertson, another City man and already a noted poet by the age of 24. His name appears on the Thiepval Memorial to the Missing.

As you proceed along the track, the tree line comes closer to it until the old front line can be seen behind the fence. There, at the forward edge of the trees, is a large cement cross. It commemorates Private A E Bull of the Sheffield City battalion who was killed on 1st July but whose body was discovered at this spot as late as April 1928; he was then buried in Serre No 2 Cemetery. This area is Mark Copse, from which came the Accrington Pals on 1st July.

Follow the grass path on your left through the field towards Queens Cemetery. In this direction came 10/RWF on 13th November led by Captain Rudd and Captain Bishop. They went to within a hundred yards of the village only to be swallowed up and killed. Behind them came 1/Gordons, struggling in their kilts in the deep mud, with only a few getting through to the Welshmen. **Walk around the back** of the cemetery and **another two hundred yards east** towards Serre and you will be on the approximate site of the German front line. You can then appreciate the strength of their position and the view that they had over the British lines.

Queens Cemetery is almost a square, in the middle of No Man's Land in the front of Mark Copse. There are 311 burials, 131 of which are unidentified. 55 of

Luke Copse British Cemetery with an unusual headstone layout.

the identified came from the Accringtons and 33 from the Sheffield City battalion. There are a couple of 18 year old men here, both from the Pals, Private C Davison of the Leeds and Private W Singleton of the Accringtons. Amongst the officers buried here is Captain A B Tough of the Accringtons. He led his men in the first wave out of Mark Copse at 7.20 am. He was almost immediately wounded but carried on to lie down a hundred yards from the British line; at 7.30 am, as the rest of the battalion came on, he stood up to urge his men forward and was shot and killed.

Return to the track by the trees and go through a gate and down some steps into the Sheffield Memorial Park. Small wooden plaques have been affixed to some of the trees to commemorate Pals battalions or companies. Ahead is a small brick and stone pavilion with seats from which to contemplate the scene. To the left, on the front line, is the new and striking memorial to the Accrington Pals, a tribute to the likes of people such as Bill Turner who have in recent times worked so diligently to ensure that the memory of these men from Accrington is not forgotten. Part of BBC's *Songs of Praise* was broadcast from here at the time of the unveiling of the memorial. **Walking down the hill,** and noting the remnants of shell holes and craters round about, you come to the bottom of the valley and Railway Hollow Cemetery. Look beyond it to the ridge above and a stand of trees and a modern brick shed is all that remains of Touvent Farm. It was there that Sergeant Smith of 1/5 LF won his DCM in August 1918. The farm was one of the major objectives in the attack of June 1915.

Railway Hollow Cemetery is hidden from the track in front of the woods. It lies in the bottom of the valley where ran Rob Roy trench and the support lines for both battles of 1916. It holds 103 British soldiers from those battles and two Frenchmen from the 1915 battle. There are three from the probes of February 1917 by 1/North Staffs and 10/Worcs, although there are also 44 unidentified. The approach to the cemetery, across a short stretch of field, is often rather muddy, and this gives the smallest inkling of the conditions that existed here in November 1916, when the trenches at the bottom of the valley were running streams and where men were trapped in the mud. All along the valley and down its sides were trenches, filled with thousands of men; as they rose from them in a cloud of artillery fire and a hail of bullets the casualties would have littered the ground. This horrific scene is such a contrast to the peace and tranquillity that is the characteristic of this place today.

Return to the track in front of the line of trees and continue along it up the hill. On your way up, about halfway along to the next cemetery on the eastern top of the valley, stop and look back to your right. To the left of the wood some few hundred yards, on the western side of the valley floor, was Matthew Copse, which was not reinstated after the war. Further over to the left and at the top of the far slope is La Signy Farm which features in all of the battles. It was from here that Lieutenant Penna and some of the pioneers from 20/KRRC worked to keep the railway operational during the battle of 13th November, and whose labour doubtless saved the lives of many of the wounded who would otherwise have had to wait many hours before they could have been removed from the cauldron of battle. In the middle of the far slope is all that remains of Observation Wood, from which the brigadiers in their dugout watched the carnage before them.

As you get closer to the cemetery look and see how far that section of 18/DLI came, up out of the valley alongside the Leeds Pals, penetrating four lines of German defences. They then disappeared over to the left, finding their way into Pendant Copse, 2,000 yards away on the skyline behind Serre. The dozen or so who reached that far had followed the plan to the letter.

Serre Road No 3 Cemetery stands just in No Man's Land about 50 yards from the German line and on the right flank of both the 1916 attacks. There are 81 buried here, 49 of whom are unknown. 32 of the identified soldiers took part in the 1st July attack.

Before continuing along the track, look south across the wide expanse of fields. On the skyline is the long line of trees alongside the track from Colincamps to the Sucrerie. Then halfway and to the left may be seen the pavilions of Serre Road No 2; coming nearer you may see the French Tricolour flying over their cemetery whilst closest of all, and hidden by the tall trees, is the Cross of Sacrifice inside the rear wall of Serre Road No 1. It was in the ground in front of that wall, which is where the German line was, that the right flank of the attack was ground to a halt in both July and November 1916.

As the farm at the end of the track comes closer, Ten Tree Alley and Pendant Copse become clearer. By the fence that surrounds the farm can often be found old shells, mortar bombs and grenades. At the end of the track **turn right** and head towards Serre Road No 1 and the car. On the left hand side of the road the small country lane going over the low rise towards Redan Ridge is Frontier Lane; behind it ran the very important German Serre Trench. Just beyond this was No Man's Land.

Serre Road Cemetery No 1 is the most southerly of the five cemeteries at Serre and is on the north side of the Mailly-Maillet – Puisieux road, a thousand yards from the village. It is a very large cemetery holding the graves of 2,416 soldiers, of whom 1,728 are unknown. It is a concentration cemetery, and the majority of those buried here were brought from areas not associated with the

View of the British Line from the German Front Line. In the middle distance is Queens Cemetery and in the wood is the Accrington Memorial (*left*) and the Sheffield Memorial Park.

battles for Serre. However Plot 1 Rows A to G was made by V Corps Burial Officer in May 1917, as were the other Serre cemeteries. The cemetery itself is in two Departments and three communes.

The soldiers from the 1916 battle are concentrated at the top end of the cemetery, as well as a number from New Zealand who brought the Germans to a halt in this sector in 1918. These graves are set at an angle to all the other graves in the cemetery. There are 60 identified graves from 31st Division and 107 from the 3rd. It was to this cemetery that the old comrades of the Bradford Pals used to hold a moving annual ceremony on 1st July for many years, even after World War II.

Buried in row 1A is Private Arthur Cecil Axe of the Leeds Pals, wounded in the leg within twenty yards of going over the top and subsequently dying there. He was a noted musician who played the piano on board ship during the voyage to Egypt in 1915. Lieutenant L A H Tyrrell came from the Transvaal to enlist in 8/East Yorks and Private A Greenwood left his home in Pawtucket, Rhode Island USA to join 16/West Yorks; both of them ended their days in Picardy. Two Leeds Pals buried here are notable. Lieutenant Major (his Christian name) William Booth was killed at the age of 29. He was an England and Yorkshire cricketer. Nearby is Sergeant Matthew Mossop, MM who came from Seascale, Cumberland. His tombstone is inscribed, 'One of the original Leeds Pals'.

Continue along the road to the nearby French cemetery. At Serre during that week in June 1915 their dead, wounded and missing were greater than the total of all the British battles for the village.

The cemetery rises in terraces from the main road until it reaches a long decorative wall on which there is a large bronze relief plaque. The cemetery was started by the British during the battlefield clearance at the end of the war. The French did not formally take possession of it until 1933. Engraved on the wall of the memorial are the words of a local German commander, 'You have undoubtedly sent elite troops against us. I went to the front line trench at the start of the attack and I have never seen troops who launched themselves into an attack with more courage or spirit'. Near the memorial are mass graves, one (seemingly) for officers and NCOs, another for rank and file soldiers. Although well tended some of the crosses are damaged and one or two have lost their names.

On the opposite side of the road is a chapel built in 1936. On the left hand

Left: **Private A E Bull's memorial on the edge of the Park; his remains were discovered in 1928.** *Centre*: **Sheffield Memorial Pavilion with Railway Hollow Cemetery behind.** *Right*: **The recently erected Accrington Memorial.**

Above: **Railway Hollow Cemetery just before its completion in the mid-1920s.**
Below: **From the same spot, the Cemetery in 1995.**

side of the porch is a small plaque placed here in 1964 in memory of the Germans who died here – a very unusual German memorial on the Somme. On the Sunday closest to 7th June a memorial mass is said in the chapel. It is pleasing to note that there is a local French association to perpetuate the memory of those who fought in that 1915 battle; and they are working to raise funds to restore this small chapel.

This walk ends, therefore, fittingly at the cemetery which holds so many of those Frenchmen who had fought so tenaciously to regain this part of their sacred land.

A detail from the bronze relief at the rear of the French Military Cemetery.

Park the car at the huge Serre No 2 Cemetery.

Theft from cars has been a problem in the recent past, so take all usual precautions. On most weekdays there are gardeners working in the cemetery which provides an added security.

This walk can be particularly muddy, and it gets quite windy at the top of the ridge (one can see where the name Toutvent Farm [Mighty Wind] came from), so dress accordingly.

Walk up the road towards Mailly-Maillet and after a few hundred yards, on your right, there is a good quality farm track – at least to start with. Just to its right ran a communication trench, Sackville Street, and it continued alongside for the length of the track, which then went all the way to Hebuterne; the trench changed its name as it went over the ridge to Vercingetorix. The track was cut in half by being ploughed up – this might have been due to a process called *remembrement*. Periodically, because of the complications caused by French inheritance laws, land is redivided amongst its owners by a neutral official person appointed by the civil authorities to make more economic and farming sense; as a result of fragmentation caused by bequests land can end up in scattered parcels. When this process is completed – which might happen every fifty years or so – farmers may well plough over tracks which have lost their original access purpose. This is why one often sets along a promising road or track only to find it disappearing at some very inconvenient spot for turning around!

Before you turn to go along Sackville Street, look further up the road and you will see a road marker on a pole. That marks the start of another long trench,

Serre Road No.2 Cemetery from Sackville Street.

112

Watling Street, which ran south easterly over the southern end of Redan Ridge and across the top of the famous Sunken Road in front of Beaumont (see *Somme: Beaumont Hamel*).

Sackville Street and the field to the right is where 1/8th and then 1/6 Warwicks attacked at 7.30 am on 1st July, on the right hand of the Leeds and Durham Pals. This attack, led by 1/8th Warwicks charged across the road, through the north side of the German strongpoint known as the Quadrilateral and on up Ten Tree Alley. Having lost a thousand men and both their colonels they ended up at nightfall back here and in the trenches running off it. 400 yards up the track was where the remnants of 18/DLI and the T'owd 12th, the pioneers, formed a defensive line in the street, facing Serre, in case of a German counter attack.

The wood on the left, pudding shaped and filling its hollow, is Basin Wood. Here was established a First Aid Post and a large pit dug to receive the anticipated dead. This would not have been a particularly morale boosting sight as the Accringtons and others stumbled along a 2,000 yard communication trench from Euston Dump to their place in the battle line on the evening of 30th June. Two wooden bridges had been built over the trenches, Blackfriars and Waterloo, to allow horse drawn transport to cross. La Signy Farm is off to your left, scene of so much bitter fighting.

At the track crossroads one can appreciate the strength of the position that the Germans occupied in 1915 prior to the French attack, and one can only marvel at the achievement of those French soldiers who managed to remove their enemy. 200 yards straight ahead was Red Cottage, where Battle Police would collect stragglers and forbid men to leave the battle zone without authority. This was a standard feature of all battle zones.

The track to the right no longer exists, and the best plan is to **follow the line of telegraph poles** – it comes back to life at Touvent Farm. This track was known as the Great Northern (railways again), and the trenches running down

The site of Toutvent Farm viewed from the Great Northern.

to the front line ran off it. Along it you will often find remnants of the railway line that ran on into Railway Hollow. The track was also the base of the German salient which the French eliminated in June 1915.

Over to the left is where the reserve brigades (92 in July, 9 in November 1916) awaited their summons into the battle zone. About 500 yards away on the right is a group of bushy topped trees filling a shallow hollow, Observation Wood, and the site of the Brigade Headquarters dugout. **Stand in front of it** and see their view of the battles in 1916. The hollow often contains pieces of metal and projectiles from the time of the battle.

Staff Copse was **on your left**, 300 yards further on, just over the other side of the ridge, and a few hundred yards beyond that further along the track and you will have **arrived at the small clump of trees** and brick hut that marks the site of Toutvent Farm. There are hardly any physical traces, apart from some reinforced concrete; whilst there are some remnants of very old trees, which must have been here at the time of the war. Looking towards Hebuterne on the left, one can only assume that there still remain the bodies of French and

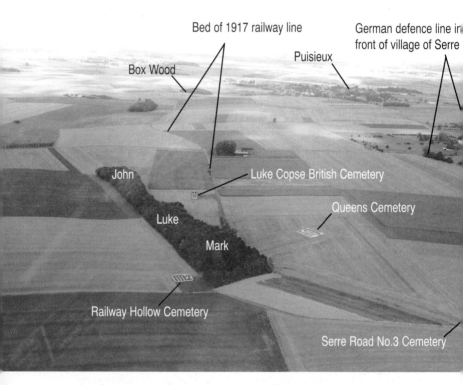

German soldiers in an area where only the plough has turned over the land. Once ringed with German defences, with extensive underground workings and the place where Lance Sergeant E Smith won the DCM in August 1918 – it is a place which is rich in bravery and heroism, with blood and tragedy.

Below you is the strip of woodland that covers the site of three of the four

'Evangelist' copses and runs along the valley floor. Stop and consider the thousands of men that came and went along the many trenches that once crisscrossed the ground. Often they would have arrived muddy and soaked, already tired from a trek through inadequate communication trenches. How much more exhausted would they be after their tour in the trenches? Then imagine the chaos of battle, men killed as they crossed trenches to get forward to the front line, the racket of gun fire – rifle, machine and artillery. All around them salvoes of shells would be falling; smoke and sometimes fog would reduce visibility. In the midst of all the din would be the shrieks of the dying and the wounded, with dismembered corpses strewing the ground and the awful disfigured, bloodied wounded either lying there or being carried to the rear. Now it is one of the most peaceful pastoral sights one could find – what a contrast!

Carry on the track for five hundred yards until you find a convenient point to **cross the field** to the northern edge of John Copse, somewhere which will not damage the crops. At the time of writing the fencing around the woods has been removed and so it is possible to walk through them and see the battered ground and indentations of trenches and dugouts. Nairne Trench ran around the northern side of the wood. Come out of the wood by Railway Hollow Cemetery, then walk up the path, through the Accringtons lines and on to the bed of the railway line that the British laid.

Look up the gradual slope and this time reflect on the Germans coming charging down the hill in August 1918, in a vain attempt to push back the advancing troops of 42nd Division. From here it is a straightforward walk back to the car at Serre Road No 2.

Serre Road Cemetery No 2 is the largest cemetery on the Somme, holding 7,139 soldiers of which only 2,295 are identified. Although the cemetery presents an open front to the road, the pavilions at the front and at the rear, along with the wall at the back, combine to produce a very noble effect. The cemetery was commenced by V Corps Burial Officer in May 1917. These 489 original burials are well up the cemetery, in Plots I and II, set at an angle, behind the War Stone and in front of the Great Cross of Sacrifice. In these plots rest many of the Warwicks who captured some of this ground on 1st July.

There are 42 soldiers identified as belonging to the three divisions that have formed the centre of our visit to Serre; they are scattered around the cemetery. Burials continued until 1934, men being brought here from miles away. One of 12/West Yorks, Pte A J Robinson, of 3rd Division was found on the battlefield in the winter of 1931-1932 and was reinterred in the special plot in front of the Thiepval Memorial, where lie 300 French and 300 British and Commonwealth soldiers as symbols of the allies who lost their lives here. On the walls of the memorial are inscribed the names of all those men from the 1916 and 1918 battles with no known graves, regiment by regiment.

When you come close to the cross you will see in front of it and slightly to the left Plot XIX. In grave E 16 is Pte Edward Albert Bull, 22, of the Sheffield Pals whose evocative memorial is on the trench in Mark Copse.

As you return to the road it is worth reflecting that on 3rd September 1944 the Guards Armoured Division came thundering along this road, 600 vehicles and tanks, in a 60 mile charge from Amiens to Douai. What were their thoughts as they charged past these 'Silent Cities'?

Start by leaving your car by the Sheffield City Memorial.

Then walk through Serre towards Puisieux. About 500 yards beyond the last house in Serre and on the right hand side, on a slow right hand bend in the road, you will see a line of thin trees and bushes and the wide entrance to a sunken lane. This is the German Flank Trench. **Proceed along the track** and after a hundred yards or so, on the right, is a wide trench entrance which snakes its way alongside the road towards Serre. It is filled with undergrowth and only in winter is it passable (and then it is muddy and slippery).

A German light railway ran along the track and into this trench, well protected by the high embankments. During the German occupation the Germans had a major Dressing Station close to this point.

On the night of 28th August Flank Trench was filled with Lancashire Fusiliers as they made their way in the dark into the trenches that came off it on either side, the Germans having withdrawn from the village to new positions further back. The Fusiliers were moving in to prepare for their next attack at 5 am the following day. A whole brigade was moved into the trenches along here, almost 2,500 men, led by 1/5th with 1/7th behind them, whilst 1/8th LF in reserve occupied the trenches closest to the German hospital.

Going along the track another 500 yards or so, and before the track begins

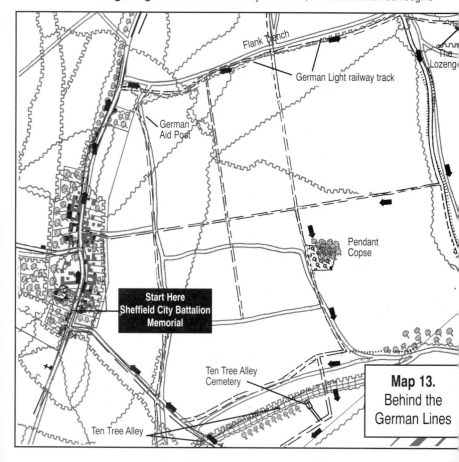

Map 13.
Behind the
German Lines

Above: **The location in Flank Trench of the German Aid Post.**
Below: **A German medical officer treats wounded in a forward Aid Post.**

to shallow, you will be approaching the headquarters of the German 169th Infantry Regiment on 1st July 1916. Get up on to the field on your left and look over the view that the Germans had over the British lines. After another 500 yards you are walking through the sunken track of Wing Trench and ahead may be seen the high banks of Puisieux Trench and the T junction with the old

Food brought up to the German front line trenches by light railway. This picture was taken on the Somme in June 1916.

Beaucourt Road. As you turn right onto the road you will see there is a track going across the gently rising plain, towards an electricity pylon standing on the highest point. In 1918 that was part of a position that the British called the Lozenge and the Germans the *Wundt Werk*. It was a machine-gun-infested strong point which Lance-Sergeant Edward Smith took at bayonet point to kill and rout the defenders, surviving the action and winning the Victoria Cross. There is no cover whatsoever, as you can see, but the high grass and dense mist obscured his charge until he was almost upon them. This was his battalion's battlefield in the division's drive for Beauregard Dovecote which now is marked by a small stand of trees 2,000 yards to the east beyond the Lozenge and to the left of the pylon. The site of the Lozenge is an outstanding battlefield viewing point.

Proceed along the road which is metalled. At its northern end it emerges at Puisieux, at its southern at Beaucourt. It is quite passable for cars except for a slightly pot holed and rutted area towards the bottom of the valley. After a while you will come to **a track on the right** which will take you up towards Pendant Copse 500 yards away. Please avoid walking in the crops when you approach it. As you come towards it, just to the east, you will have crossed Pendant Trench. The wood is covered with bracken, and again the best time to visit it is in the winter, but there are numerous shell holes and shattered remnants of trenches. You must take care of rusty barbed wire and possibly unexploded projectiles – just leave these things well alone. Somewhere around here the remnants of the attack by 18/DLI probably came to a mortal end.

Continue past the Copse and down into the valley below. Ahead of you the high bank is part of Ten Tree Alley. Above it, and sometimes concealed by the trees of the alley, is Ten Tree Alley Cemetery. The track takes you past it on its left, but you meet another track shortly, and there you will find the access path to this isolated place.

The cemetery is another one started by V Corps Burial Officer in May 1917. It stands close to Munich Trench, which was attacked by 32nd Division in November 1916 and again in February 1917, on the latter occasion alongside 62nd Division. There are only 67 graves in this tiny cemetery of whom 24 are unidentified. In the valley below the cemetery the body of a German sniper was found whilst the farmer was ploughing only some six or seven years ago. In one year his rifle, complete with sniper's accoutrements, was found; the following year his skeleton.

The track runs for 500 yards before it joins up with the Beaucourt – Serre road. **Walk back up the valley** towards Serre; where there is a track crossroad you will have arrived at Munich Trench, and where 97 Brigade came to a halt in November 1916. Between the track from the cemetery and Munich Trench you will have crossed the valley and the line of Ten Tree Alley, clearly marked by the bank and line of trees and bushes. This was the point of deepest penetration of 1/8th Warwicks on 1st July. If you look up the valley to the left you will see Serre Road No 2 a thousand yards and more away.

This gives some comprehension of what those brave Territorials achieved; and if the advance was determined, what a struggle it must have been to get back to their trenches when they had to fall back.

At the crucifix on the main road junction **turn right** and return to the car.

A few days rest out of the line for these Germans troops serving on the Somme in the spring of 1916.

Car Tour 1:   The Sucrerie and Euston Road Cemeteries, the French Battle and Roland Leighton.

This short car tour may be considered a useful respite after one of the walks; it covers the area behind the old British and French lines before Serre and the right sector of Hebuterne.

The tour commences at the Sucrerie Military Cemetery.

This is situated by a track which is off the Mailly Maillet road, just to the west of the crossroads to Auchonvillers and Colincamps. The sucrerie, or sugar factory, was on the right

The ruined French sugar factory (Sucrerie) in 1916 – behind the British lines but in range of the German guns.

as you **start down** the deeply rutted track. It is passable for a car in the right weather, but watch your sump! It is not always so easy to turn around when you reach the cemetery, especially if muddy. The cemetery is about 400 yards down the track which was an important route for soldiers coming into the battle; some of the communication trenches began in the sucrerie ruins, in particular Roman Road.

Sucrerie Military Cemetery was started by the French on the south side of a tree lined road coming down from Colincamps which is 1,000 yards or so further along. The track is now barred by a gate; it emerges in the farm of an understandably rather unsympathetic farmer. Camouflage netting hung along the edges of the road to protect its users from German artillery observers alert for any likely targets. When the British arrived it was called 10th Brigade Cemetery for a while, reflecting a 3rd Division interest. Nearly always behind allied lines the cemetery was used constantly until 26th March 1918 when the Germans overran it, but only very temporarily as they were ejected by the New Zealand Division on 28th March. Fighting actually took place in it, and 62 Kiwis are now buried here.

After the war almost 300 French and twelve German graves were removed, but only about

New Zealanders at La Signy Farm, March/April 1918, after pushing the Germans back towards Serre.

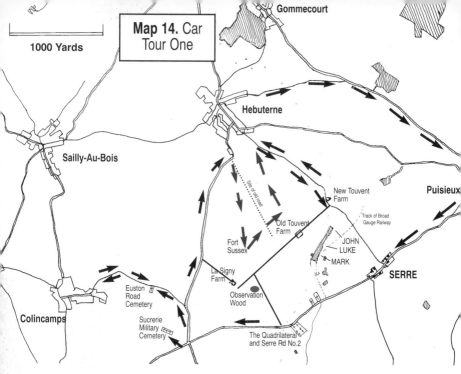

Map 14. Car Tour One

1000 Yards

Gommecourt

Hebuterne

Sailly-Au-Bois

Puisieux

New Touvent Farm

Track of Broad Gauge Railway

Old Touvent Farm

Site of old road

JOHN
LUKE
MARK

Fort Sussex

SERRE

La Signy Farm

Euston Road Cemetery

Observation Wood

Colincamps

Sucrerie Military Cemetery

The Quadrilateral and Serre Rd No.2

200 more British graves were concentrated in the cemetery. It is here that can be found some of those soldiers of 31st Division killed before 1st July in trench raids, bombardments and by snipers – so called trench wastage. There are 163 men brought in from the battlefield, just over a mile away. Many of them are Leeds Pals. Private J N Sen was killed on 22nd May 1916 when, after a clash in No Man's Land, the battalion was subjected to a terrific bombardment. He had come from Bengal to Leeds University and after taking a degree in Engineering was employed by the Corporation. Typical of many who had secure and quite senior jobs, he volunteered in September 1914; he was 29 when he was killed. His Company Sergeant Major, J W Ellis, was killed on 4th May.

Eighteen soldiers of 42nd (East Lancs) Division have their final resting place here, killed in the summer months before they finally shifted the Germans from Serre. Two battalion commanders killed on 1st July in the attack on Redan Ridge are buried side by side. The Hon Lawrence Palk DSO and Legion of Honour commanded 1/Hants. John Thicknesse commanded 1/Somersets; his military career had taken him to the North West Frontier of India,

Trench narrow guage railway systems were constructed behind the lines by both sides.

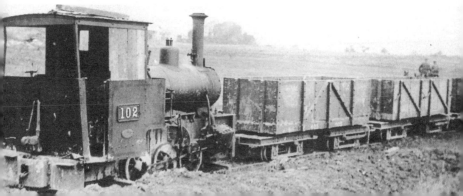

and he had fought in the South African Campaign. Battalions often considered it a matter of honour to try and retrieve the bodies of their officers, and this was particularly true of their Commanding Officer.

The lane had numerous dugouts carved out nearby. By looking north Hebuterne can be seen on its small hill and slightly to the left about half a mile away is the Cross of Sacrifice in Euston Road Cemetery.

Return to the main road and turn left and **then left again** on the D129 towards Colincamps. Within a short distance the road forks: **keep left**. A large store dump, full of barbed wire, sandbags and the like, was placed nearby, hence Euston Dump. The trench railway ran close by, which gave rise to names such as Euston, Blackfriars, Waterloo Bridge and Railway Avenue for features and trenches in the immediate vicinity.

The cemetery first came into use in the battle of 1st July. After the Germans retreated it was not used again until 1918. In the German offensive of that year both it and Colincamps further west were overrun, but were recaptured by 14 Whippet tanks of the 8th Battalion New Zealand Tank Corps, followed by 2/Auckland Rifles. It figured prominently in a German attack on 3 New Zealand (Rifle) Brigade on 5th April 1918.

All of the graves made during the war are in Plot 1, some of them tightly packed. Afterwards 758 soldiers were concentrated here, filling in the space between the original plot and the road; bodies were brought from, amongst other places, John Copse 1 and 2 Cemeteries which were off the Serheb Road and from Lonely Cemetery which was close to Central Avenue a few hundred yards to the north. It contained 17 New Zealand graves.

There are two rows of Special Memorials just inside the gate, one of which commemorates Sergeant J W Streets of 12/York & Lancs (Sheffield City Battalion) who was last seen, already wounded, going into No Man's Land to rescue a badly wounded man of his platoon. He was a coal miner and a noted poet who is best known for his poem 'Comrades'.

Of the original 501 graves in Plot 1, 312 are from 31st and 3rd divisions; 117 are soldiers killed on 1st July from 31st Division. The majority of the 195 burials from the November battle were members of 12 and 13/East Yorks. The youngest from these battalions is Pte L Cullum of 13/East Yorks, aged 18. He is buried just

Sergeant John William Streets

inside the gate on the right, and was one of those brought here after the war. There is an Indian soldier buried in the cemetery, Driver Lekha, a Punjabi from Ambala who died on 2nd September 1918. It is a mystery as to how he came to be with the Ammunition Column of 42nd Division.

Proceed into Colincamps. This is a small village, and like so many on the Somme is very quiet – it is rare to see any people on the streets. It was completely destroyed during the war, the *coup de grace* coming with the fighting of 1918.

Return to Euston and take a **left turn at the fork**, heading towards Hebuterne. From this road it is possible to get a good view over the country across which the French attacked in June 1915. The road is wide enough for you to stop periodically and look over to the east. The large farm on your right is La Signy Farm. The attack began on 9th June from its access track to this road and the Mailly Maillet – Serre road. It was the third of the French attacks on the Toutvent Farm salient in three days, each from a different angle. The attack was delayed until 5 pm because of the poor weather, and then continued until the evening of 11th June. The French gradually worked their way to the line that was to become the British one a month or so later.

Proceed about 400 yards further down the road, which is near the site of Fort Southdown, a strong point in the rear of the British line, and not far from the exit point of Palestine Trench, an important communication trench. The small stand of trees and, in the right season, the small brick hut that stands on the site of Toutvent Farm should be seen almost directly east of you about 2,000 yards away. The French attacked the Farm from a start point to the west of the road, on a 2,000 yard front. This onslaught was on 7th June, the first of the series of French attacks. The north point of this attack front was a feature called the Quarries, which is marked on the modern IGN map as *la Briqueterie*, on a slight right hand bend about 600 yards from Hebuterne. It is a good point as well to look at the whole of the German position to the east, with the church spires of Puisieux and Bucquoy visible to the north east and the high ground before Serre to the east.

De Castelnau resumed the offensive on this part of the attack front on 13th June, and the French succeeded in pushing the Germans back to their Second Line defences, which became their new line, the one which faced the incoming British. The third phase of the French attack, on 8th June, will be viewed later.

Continue into Hebuterne; on the southern outskirts of the village there is a crossroads, the main road bending around to the left. On your right there is a rural lane, and beside it, on the left, is the communal cemetery.

This is a moving spot, as there are numbers of both French and British military graves – 60 or so British and probably twice that number of French. It symbolises the sacrifice of both nations on this part of the front. On the right hand side there is a group of half a dozen Gunners, from A Battery 170 Bde Field Artillery, presumably the victims of a German shell on their emplacement or some similar disaster; they all died on 21st October 1916. Further over on the right is the (civil) grave of a Don Cossack – one wonders what his story was.

Proceed down the country road, which takes you almost due south. A communication trench called *Vercingetorix* ran alongside on the left. After three quarters of a mile or so there is another reasonable driving surface on the left; it might be wise to stop the car here. This is the approximate position of Fort Sussex, another strong point and communication trench crossway. It is tucked away in a fold in the ground. Continue along the original track on foot; this eventually dies out altogether, more or less where the police post at Red Cottage used to stand. The Great Northern is visible, running from right to left, with La Signy Farm a few hundred yards away on your right and Toutvent Farm 800 yards or so on your left, with Observation Wood visible a few hundred yards before that.

Proceed left along the track, now heading northeast. The second road that came south from Hebuterne crossed about 400 yards along here. This was almost certainly the track which the ambulance used to remove Roland Leighton to Louvencourt. Stop where it makes a sharp turn to the left. About three hundred yards to your right is the site of Toutvent Farm; note the quite appreciable slope leading up to it. About 300 yards to the west of it is the site of Staff Copse, now gone. To the east of your position, almost straight in front of you and about 600 yards away, is New Toutvent Farm, situated in a dip in the ground. The new farm has retained the British spelling.

Just to the right of the road was a communication trench called *Jean Bart*. This is quite probably the trench along which Leighton was carried to a dressing station that was close to the British cemetery in Hebuterne. The now ploughed over road came out at its southern end onto the Great Northern, a hundred yards or so to the south west of Staff Copse. Chasseurs Hedge (that hedge mentioned in Robert Leighton's account) came off Jean Bart Trench, about

250 yards south east of your present position, and it then ran on eastwards to the front line just before New Touvent Farm.

Proceed north on the road, joining Serheb road just before Hebuterne. **Turn right** and proceed as far as New Toutvent Farm. **Park on the right hand side**, just beyond it, on the track that used to run up to its old site along the Great Northern.

The British line was on the east side of the road near where you have parked your car, and the front of the present farm stands on that position. Just beyond the farm the line twisted sharply westwards, to your left as you **walk up to it**. Where the road makes a similar sharp turn, and about fifty yards further north, was a German position called The Point, with a sap running out southwards towards the British line. The German sniper that shot Leighton was positioned about fifty yards to the southeast of The Point. **Returning to the car**, Leighton received his mortal wound somewhere in the vicinity of the farm courtyard and outer buildings. By the new barn door a stack of munitions are usually sitting awaiting disposal.

Return towards Hebuterne on the Serheb Road and **take a small turning to the right** just before entering the village. **Turn right again at a T Junction**, which will put you on the D27 for Puisieux. Proceed until you come to a quarry on your left hand side, although notice the demarcation stone, also on your left, several hundred yards before it. It has a French helmet on it, indicating that it was their troops that halted the German advance at this point. It is in the wrong place, as the Germans were actually in Hebuterne in 1918 and were stopped by the New Zealand Division. **Get out of the car** and look back about three hundred yards. This is the approximate site of La Louvière Farm, which stood adjacent to the left hand side of the road.

The French launched their attack on the line before La Louvière Farm and to the north of New Toutvent Farm on 8th June at 3 am; the attack did not do particularly well, but this second blow in force made the Germans concerned about the strength of the French attack and their possible intentions.

Proceed from the quarry towards Hebuterne. After a few hundred yards you will notice trees and bushes stretching out south westwards on your right hand side. **Proceed another hundred yards** or so and **stop by a track that leads off to the right**. This track was the bed of the broad gauge railway that continues past the copses at Serre. It is an interesting walk in its own right. **Proceed on foot** back to the trees mentioned above; taking all due precautions against barbed wire, hunters and the like, you will find the remnants of a German defence system, quite distinct, which may be followed – undergrowth allowing – for a few hundred yards. This was part of their second line defence system, and runs into Star Wood.

Continue into Puisieux; if you need refreshment the nearest cafe is in Bucquoy. The far end of this town also boasts a handy supermarket, which has a petrol station attached which sells fuel at the cheapest prices I have found in the area.

125

This tour is designed to take you over the areas and villages that were used by the troops as billets and concentration points; where headquarters were established; where the artillery and other arms in the divisions fought and served; and where sadly in many cases men found their final resting place.

This tour starts in Albert; **proceed towards Amiens**, but whilst still in the town take a **right hand turn**, the **D938 to Doullens**.

This soon passes under a railway bridge. Just before Hedauville, some five miles out of Albert, a stand was made by the British in 1940 against the German advance. Over five hundred years earlier Henry V's army also crossed nearby, on its way to Agincourt. Two miles beyond Hedauville (after you have passed through Forceville) you will arrive at Acheux-en-Amienois. Coming close to this large village you will see, on the right, a large wood. It was here that the tanks were concentrated prior to the Battle of the Ancre in November 1916. At the centre of the village there is a **turning to the left**, which has a sign for Acheux Military Cemetery. The Commonwealth War Graves Cemeteries are usually well signposted, but sometimes the distinctive green signs edged in white are obscured by other signs, a building or vegetation, so keep alert. The cemetery is set back from the road on the right hand side.

VIII Corps Collection Station was established at Acheux in readiness for the Battle of the Somme in 1916. Private John Crerar (18/West Yorks), who came from Bradford, died of gas poisoning in September 1916. In 1918 the German line came within five miles of the village, and the cemetery, which had not been used after the German retreat to the Hindenburg Line, once more came into operation for a few of the summer months of 1918.

Return to the crossroads in Acheux and **turn left** for Louvencourt, about two miles away. Louvencourt Military Cemetery is on the edge of the village from this direction, down a **minor road on the left** hand side.

This is a most unusual cemetery because of the unique French gravestones – large

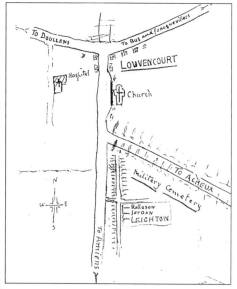

and imposing, with a helmet in relief at the top, but with little more information on them about the soldier buried than is found on the usual French crosses. British Field Ambulances were established here on the departure of the French from the sector in July 1915 – the sketch by Robert Leighton shows the location of the hospital.

Roland Leighton's grave is on the left as you enter the cemetery.

Note that the sketch is inaccurate about the positioning of Roland Leighton's and the other two graves of 1/7th Worcesters officers.

Captain A G Rollason died of pneumonia on 30th July 1915, soon after the battalion

126

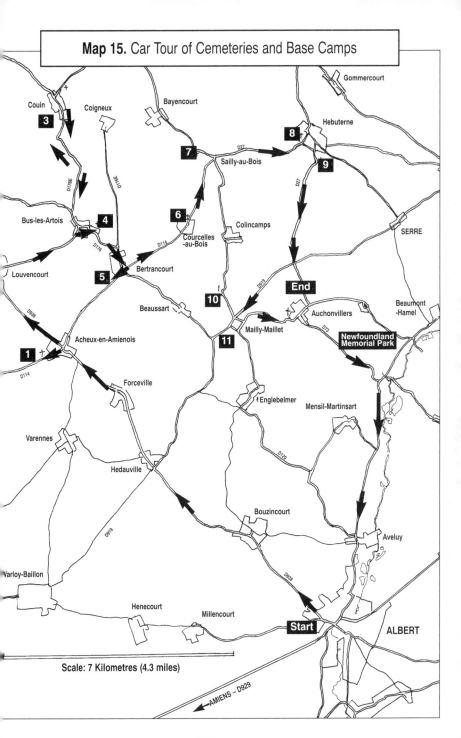

Map 15. Car Tour of Cemeteries and Base Camps

Gommercourt

Couin

Coigneux

Bayencourt

3

Hebuterne

8

D27

7

Sailly-au-Bois

9

D27

Bus-les-Artois

4

D176E

D176E

6

Colincamps

SERRE

D114

Courcelles
-au-Bois

Louvencourt

D176

5

Bertrancourt

D919

End

Beaumont
-Hamel

D638

Beaussart

10

Auchonvillers

Acheux-en-Amienois

Mailly-Maillet

D73

1

11

Newfoundland
Memorial Park

D114

Forceville

Englebelmer

Mensil-Martinsart

Varennes

D129

Hedauville

Bouzincourt

D919

Aveluy

Varloy-Baillon

D938

Henecourt

Millencourt

Start

ALBERT

Scale: 7 Kilometres (4.3 miles)

AMIENS – D929

127

Brigadier-General Prowse

arrived in front of Hebuterne. Second-Lieutenant John Jordan died of disease in February 1916. Almost half of the graves date from the 1918 fighting. The most prominent soldier buried here is Brigadier-General Charles Bertie Prowse, DSO who was killed on 1st July 1916 whilst commanding 11 Brigade. He received his fatal wounds in the area of the Quadrilateral. A member of the Somerset Light Infantry, there is an unusual brass plaque placed on his grave: 'As a tribute to his memory from his Old Comrades of the 7th Bn Somerset LI.' He has another unusual distinction, that is, a cemetery named after him. This is Prowse Point Military Cemetery, on the northern edge of Ploegsteert Wood near the hamlet of St Yvon.

Prowse was originally buried, along with seven others, in Vauchelles-les-Authie, a mile along the road to Doullens, in a Communal Cemetery Extension; these are all now in Row E. This was for the Field Ambulances that were stationed there, but these were the only burials that took place. Captain Edward Gatacre died in February 1916. It is interesting to note that his regiment – 2/Duke of Wellingtons – was good at rugby even at the turn of the century. He was Captain of the Regimental team, which he led to victory in the Calcutta Cup between 1907 - 1910. He was also a member of the Guard of Honour at the Delhi Durbar in 1911.

Two Leeds Pals, Privates Cockroft and Mackin were killed together on 22nd December and are buried side by side in Plot 1, Row D.

Louvencourt is a quiet village and still has a number of old barns which old soldiers might recognise – or at least their building style. It was in this village that the Accrington Pals assembled after their efforts on 1st July, with only a small proportion of those who had set out to answer the roll. It must have been a heartbreaking occasion.

Farm at Bus-Les-Artois where, on the eve of the 'Big Push', an accident occured in which one man was killed and fourteen others were seriously injured. D Company of the Leeds Pals was parading in the courtyard and Private Henderson began to redistribute his load of hand grenades when two them exploded.

Still in existence after 80 years a 31st (Pals) Division sign, painted in the spring of 1916, on a wall in the village of Couin.

Return to the main road and take the **minor road on the right** at the bottom of the hill **after the church**. After a couple of miles Bus-les-Artois is reached. There is no military cemetery here, but in the surrounding fields, woods and houses of the village were housed members of the divisions that attacked at Serre. It was subject to intermittent shelling from long range artillery, but it was generally a safe place; the consequent disadvantage was that the march to and from the line was long.

In one of the courtyards in the village, on the evening of 31st June, just before the Leeds Pals marched off to the battle, there was a serious accident. Private Robert Henderson was priming grenades and passing them amongst some of the men when one was triggered off which killed him and wounded many others. There are two British soldiers buried at the far end of Bus Communal Cemetery, which is off the main road on the right, just before the church. They were both killed on 21st August 1916, members of 2 Guards Brigade.

Return to the road and proceed to Couin, taking the **right hand D176e** at the far end of the village. This village is built on the slope of a steep valley. At a cross roads in the village note, on the right hand side, an old brick wall which still carries the legend 'Water Point' in large lettering of white paint. It would seem that someone has painted it since the war, as it is in remarkably good condition. Proceed past the church and the high walls of a semi-derelict chateau and take a turning to the right which does not have a CWGC sign. After a kilometre or so you will come to two British cemeteries on either side of the road; Couin British and Couin New British Cemeteries.

Couin British Cemetery was started by Field Ambulances attached to 48th (South Midland) Division in May 1916. It was closed at the end of January 1917 because it was full. One of the last to be buried here was Brigadier-General Walter Long, CMG, DSO who was killed in action at Hebuterne in January 1917. He was hit by a shell in the trenches near Yankee Street, close to the present site of Gommecourt British Cemetery No 2. He won his DSO during the Boer war, afterwards serving as ADC to the Governor General of Canada. He took command of his brigade in November 1916, and was killed whilst inspecting the trenches. He was the son of Rt Hon Walter Long, Secretary of State for the Colonies at the time of his death and his mother was the daughter of 9th Earl of Cork and Orerry. Private B Gambles of 12/York & Lancs (Sheffield City Battalion) died of his wounds on 1st July 1916 which he received in action on 28th June whilst bringing in a wounded comrade from a raid. Captain Basil Hallam Radford of the Royal Flying Corps was killed when he fell from his observation balloon in August 1916. He is rather better known for the Music Hall number, 'Gilbert the Filbert, the Knut with a K'. Beyond this cemetery, hidden amongst the woods, is Couin Chateau, used by the British as a divisional headquarters between 1915 and 1918 .

Opposite is Couin New British Cemetery. Amongst those buried here is Lieutenant John Bernard Pye Adams who died of wounds on 27th February 1917. He was a member of the Royal Welch Fusiliers (1st Battalion), and knew both Sasoon and Graves. His legacy is an outstanding autobiographical account of his war, written whilst he was recovering from wounds received above Fricourt where he was the sniping officer. Sassoon was somewhat patronising about this book, *Nothing of Importance*, but to my mind it is one of the finest books of its type and, especially for anyone visiting the Fricourt part of the line, well worth a read. It was reprinted several years ago and is often to be found in second hand lists. Also buried here is Sergeant Richard Charles Travis (his real name was Dickson Cornelius Savage), VC, DCM, MM, Croix de Guerre (Belgium) of 2nd Bn Otago Regiment NZEF.

He was killed in action on 25th July 1918. He was known as 'Prince of Scouts' and 'King of No Man's Land'. He won the VC posthumously.

'For most conspicuous bravery and devotion to duty. During 'surprise' operations it was necessary to destroy an impassable wire block [this is in the vicinity of Rossignol Wood]. Sgt Travis, regardless of personal danger, volunteered for this duty. Before zero hour, in broad daylight and in close proximity to enemy posts he crawled out and successfully destroyed the block with bombs, thus enabling the attacking party to pass through. A few minutes later a bombing party on the right of the attack was held up by two machine guns, and the success of the whole operation was in danger. Perceiving this Sgt Travis with great gallantry and utter disregard of danger, rushed the position, killed the crews and captured the guns. An enemy officer and three men immediately rushed at him from a bend in the trench and attempted to retake the guns. These four he killed single handed, thus allowing the bombing party on which much depended to advance. The success of this operation was almost entirely due to the heroic work of this gallant NCO and the vigour with which he made and used opportunities for inflicting casualties on the enemy. He was killed 24 hours later when, in a most intense bombardment prior to an enemy counter attack, he was going from post to post to encourage the men.'

Return to Bus and take the road to Bertrancourt. At the centre of Betrancourt take the **right hand turn to Acheux**. After a short distance there is a **right hand turn** to Bertrancourt Military Cemetery, indicated by a CWGC sign. The cemetery, after a few hundred yards, is on the left hand side, down a long grass path.This is a cemetery in two

Above: **Sailly-Au-Bois Church was used by 42nd Division. Catacombs in the area were also used by various units.**
Inset: **The church in 1918 as the war ended.**

parts. The further plot consists in the main of 1916 burials, whilst Plot II, nearest to the gates, those from 1918. In this plot are 117 territorials of 42nd (East Lancs) Division. There are also 90 men from 31st and 3rd divisions; amongst them in Plot I is the adjutant of the Leeds Pals, Captain Edward Karl de Pledge, killed on 3rd June 1916. The oldest soldiers of 31st Division buried anywhere near the old front are both here – Private T James of the Barnsley Pals, killed 13th June 1916 aged 47 and Sergean B Moseley of 'T'owd 12th', a pioneer from Wakefield, killed on 4th July 1916, aged 48. At the opposite end of the age range are two 17 year old boys, Private J W Hirst of 16/West Yorks, killed on 13th June 1916 and Private W Gaskell of 1/7th Lancashire Fusiliers who died of wounds on 14th August 1918.

Returning to Bertrancourt, there is a cafe near the French War Memorial should restorative action be required.

Take the D114 (straight on at the crossroads) for Courcelles-au-Bois and to Courcelles-au-Bois Communal and Communal Cemetery Extension. These cemeteries are on the road out to Sailly-au-Bois.

The area through which you have travelled was filled with all types of artillery during the war. The village was a halfway house to the front line at Serre, some 4,000 yards away, and battalions assembled here on their way to the line. It was also a place of importance to the 42nd Division in the summer of 1918, as they gradually ground their way forward to Serre.

In the Communal Cemetery there are three British soldiers buried (all on the western edge), casualties from September 1916. There are five French soldiers here as well, from the fighting of the preceding year. The extension was opened in the October of 1916.

The gravestones are all red, an experiment with a different type of stone in an attempt by the CWGC to ease maintenance costs.

Of the 115 graves, 23 are from 3rd Division, including four pioneers from 20/KRRC who were casualties in the November fighting, valiantly trying to maintain the railway and communications. What is notable is the large number of gunners – victims of the German counter-battery work.

Sailly-au-Bois is a **mile to the north east**; the land, especially on the right, was regularly occupied by artillery pieces during the Somme battles. The village was transformed into ruins during the battle, being only 4000 yards or so from the front. Troops still tried to find shelter there, as well as in the neighbouring fields and woodland. After the war the village was adopted by Hastings.

31st Division was brought slightly to the west of here in support of 3rd Division in November 1916. When the latter was withdrawn after the hard battle of that month, the 31st was moved to Bus, three miles to the south west. In the summer of 1918 it was the turn of the 42nd Division to occupy the village; the church was on the left flank of its 3000 yard front. The church has of course been restored, but the crypt was used by successive battalions of the division as their headquarters.

Below the church, **take the D23 signposted Souastre** (the CWGC sign can be a little difficult to find) and on the outer edge of the village, on the left hand side of the road and on a bank, is Sailly-au-Bois Military Cemetery. It was begun in May 1916 'in a field opposite the town major's dugout'. That dugout would now seem to be under a new house. All of those buried here are known, which betrays its origins as a Field Ambulance hospital. Most of those here would have died of wounds, either at the hospital or en route from the trenches. 46 of the dead are Gunners and 83 are from 31st Division, with all of its battalions represented. 18/West Yorks alone have 24 of their Pals here; there are 11 Accrington Pals. Private G Robson of the Leeds Pals won the MM for his bravery at Serre in July, only to be killed a few months later, on 23rd November 1916. He was an original

Horse lines out of range of German artillery in June 1915. Hebuterne was well within range and horses were easy victims.

Hebuterne Church as it was in 1915 and today.

Pal and was only 20 years old.

Take the D27 to Hebuterne. This road, slightly winding and rising, open on both sides, was under easy German observation and frequently shelled. The verges were littered with dead horses, smashed carts and other vehicles. On the left of the road there were numerous horse lines.

Hebuterne is a large but quiet village, adopted by Evesham because of its association with battalions of the Worcesters which served in 48th (South Midland) Division. Because it was so close to the front it had its own defence system. The streets were barricaded and trenches ran parallel to the main road.

Hebuterne Military Cemetery is reached as you enter the village at a crossroads of tracks and metalled roads. The CWGC sign can get lost in the undergrowth. Take the left-hand turn and proceed along a narrow road for a few hundred yards. The cemetery is on your right, but well set back, so look out for a set of stairs leading up to the path to the cemetery. If you are thinking of picnicking, this is the cemetery that I would recommend – it is beautiful and peaceful, and there are plenty of interesting inscriptions amongst the 700 and more soldiers buried here.

The burials took place throughout the British occupation of the sector by the British; it was started by 48th Division in August 1915. The cemetery has irregular rows, a consequence of the nature of the burials over the years. It makes an interesting instruction in the progress of the war to walk amongst the graves and see some of the plots established by the various divisions. There are three Germans buried in the cemetery. For a time in 1918 the Germans occupied part of the village; the cemetery was

Above: **The 1/8 Royal Warwickshire Regiment in trenches in front of Hebuterne. The soldier is operating a home made shooting device with periscope attached.** *(Terry Carter)*
Below: **Officer of the Royal Warwickshire's using a sniping rifle. Note the spotter's telescope to his right.** *(Terry Carter)*

Looking towards the village of Serre from the trenches in front of Hebuterne in 1915. The shattered trees of one of the copses (likely John Copse) in the middle distance. *(Terry Carter)*

certainly damaged during the fighting. 45 of the graves are of unknown soldiers, but 17 of them are commemorated on special memorials, as they are known to be buried here. Two American soldiers who were in the cemetery served with the New Zealand Division whilst their regiment was on attachment; their graves have been removed, possibly to the American Somme Cemetery.

Amongst the 53 New Zealanders buried here is Captain Richard Seddon, who was born in 1881. His father was Rt Hon Richard Seddon, PC LL.D, who was Prime Minister of New Zealand from 1893 - 1906. His son had also fought in the South African campaign.

Drive into Hebuterne and turn right. Take a **right hand turn** (D27) immediately after the church and after five hundred yards or so note the Communal Cemetery on the left. **Proceed into Mailly-Maillet** and in the village, at the **traffic lights**, take the **right hand** turn for Sailly-au-Bois. The cemetery is on a road off to the left, up the side of the valley, about a kilometre or so along this road, beyond the edge of the village. Mailly-Maillet Communal Cemetery Extension is a small rectangular cemetery, originally started by the French, but their 51 graves (mainly Engineers) have been removed. There are three rows; two 1st Barnsley Pals are amongst those here.

Private JC Ackroyd was killed on 14th May, only a few weeks after arriving from Egypt, and almost opposite him is Private A Naylor, killed on 21st June 1916.

Return to the village and turn right, following the road to Forceville.

As you leave the village, on the left, you will see a high wall.

Mailly Wood Cemetery is up a track on the left more or less where this wall stops – this warning to prevent you overshooting. The track is managable for the first part, but you might wish to walk the last hundred yards or so. This cemetery was used extensively by

51st (Highland) Division after their successful attack on Beaumont Hamel on 13th November 1916. [see *Beaumont Hamel* in the same series]. Amongst those buried here is Sergeant H Colley VC, MM of 10/Lancs Fusiliers. Private C W Newcomb MM of 1/5th Manchesters was killed near Serre on 15th August 1918. He was a veteran of Gallipoli.

Return to Mailly-Maillet and take a **right hand turn**, the D129 towards Englebelmer. At the church **turn left**, but before doing so try and find a place to stop and admire the richly ornate west end of the entrance to the church. It is nothing short of miraculous that this important piece of art was preserved from the destruction of the fighting. The whole thing was encased in sand bags to protect it during the war. **Follow the road** to Auchonvillers and you will find shortly after entering the village, on your left-hand side, a guest house where you can find a welcome from Avril Williams and a drink and an opportunity to visit fascinating cellars used as a dressing station during the war.

Cemetery at Mailly-Maillet at the end of the war.

12th Battalion York & Lancaster Regiment
Sheffield City Battalion

BATTALION WAR DIARY EXTRACT
Saturday 1st July, 1916
1.40 am to 7.30 am

———

All battalions in the British Army (beginning with the First World War), keep a day to day diary of events apertaining to their unit during periods of active service. The amount of detail given, and consequently their value to researchers and historians, depends very much on the individual journalistic ability of the battalion diarist. Copies of the diaries are lodged with the regimental museums and at the Central Records Office at Kew Gardens.

The three pages here extracted from the 12th Battalion York & Lancaster Regiment represent the very best record keeping for a unit in action, and give in graphic detail the events of the hours leading up to, and those disastrous opening minutes of, the Battle of the Somme.

This extract should be read in conjunction with *The Death of Innocence* beginning page 49.

Summary of Events and Information

Place	Date	Hour	Summary of Events and Information
COLINCAMPS SECTOR	1.7.16	1.40am	Battalion Headquarters consisting of Major A.Plackett,Commanding;Major A R Hoette,second-in-Command;Captain & Adjutant N.L.Tunbridge,Lieutenant H. Oxley,Signalling Officer,and other Headquarters' Details arrived at JOHN Copse. All quiet.Nothing seen of "A" & "C" Companies.
〃	〃	1.55am	Captain Clarke reported our own wire cut on our front and tapes laid out in front of our line,vide Battalion Operation Order,No.15,para.2 (a,b,o,d.) Laying of tape completed about 12-30. am.Report sent to Brigade Hdqtrs in DUNMOW.
〃	3〃	2.40am	The first and second waves of "A" Coy reported in position in the Assembly trenches.Company Hdqtrs established in the front line near its junction with JORDAN.
〃	〃	2.45am	Lieut.ELAM reported Battalion in position in the Assembly trenches.Reports not yet received from "B","C",& "D" Coys,however.
〃	〃	3.50am	"D" Coy reported in position.
〃	〃	4.5am	Enemy started shelling JOHN COPSE and front line.
〃	〃	5.25am	Report sent to 94th Infantry Brigade.Battalion in position in Assembly trenches.
〃	〃	6.0am	"C" Company report our own guns firing short on the front line between JOHN & LUKE COPSES causing casualties. Reported to Brigade by runner telephonic communication being out.
〃	〃	6.30am	"C" Coy reported Bays 31 to 38 heavily shelled.8 killed & 6 wounded—principally No 12 platoon. Reply sent "Report again at 7-0 am.Nothing can be done at present."
〃	〃	7.0am	"C" Coy reported no further casualties ,but that our guns had been firing short, and had been hitting our own parapet in the front line.This was reported to Brigade.
			NOTES: The Communication trenches i.e.,NORTHERN AVENUE,PYLON,& NAIRNE were in an exceedingly bad condition owing to the heavy rain;in places the water

2449 Wt. W4957/M90 750,000 1/16 J.B.C.& A. Forms/C.2118/12

Place	Date	Hour	Summary of Events and Information

Summary of Events and Information

COLIN CAMPS. SECTOR.

was well above the knees. This caused great fatigue to the men and consequently delayed assembly of Battalion in the trenches at least 2½ hours.

The Eastern end of NAIRNB was found to be considerably blown in, but was passable. The front line was badly smashed up throughout its length; also the Traffic trench. COPSE trench was also badly smashed up. MONK & CAMPION were in a bad state, but this was due to the weather rather than to the enemy shelling.

From the outset telephonic communication with the Brigade was cut, and the only means of communication throughout the day was by runner.

The enemy artillery continued shelling heavily from 4.5 am, until the attack commenced. In view of the fact that the enemy artillery became active as soon as it was daylight, it would appear likely that the enemy was warned of the attack by observing gaps out in our own wire and tapes laid out in No Man's Land, thus obtaining at least three and a half hours warning of the attack.

"A" Coy reported no sign of the tape which was laid during the night; it had, apparently, been removed. It served no purpose at all except to give the enemy warning.

The wire in front of our lines had been cut away too much and as the gaps were not staggered, our intention to attack must have been quite obvious to the enemy.

| | 1.7.16 | 7.20ᴬᴹ | The first wave of "A" and "C" proceeded into No Man's Land and laid down about 100 yards in front of our trenches under cover of intense bombardment by Stokes Mortars and Artillery. Casualties were not heavy up to this point. |
| | 1.7.16 | 7.29ᴬᴹ | Second wave moved forward and took up a position about 30 yards in rear of the first wave. The third and fourth waves left CAMPION & MONK and advanced in first wave. The enemy started an artillery barrage commencing at MONK section columns. The enemy started an artillery barrage commencing at MONK and gradually rolling forward to the front line, where it finally settled . |

i 449 Wt. W14957/M90 750,000 1/16 J.B.C. & A. Forms/C.2118/12.

Summary of Events and Information

Place	Date	Hour	
COLINCAMPS SECTOR	1/7/16	7.20	

Barrage lifted from the German front line and first and second waves moved forward to the assault. They were immediately met with very heavy machine gun and rifle and fire and artillery barrage. The left half of "C" Coy was wiped out before getting near the German wire, and on the right the few men who reached the wire were unable to get through. As soon as our barrage lifted from their front line, the Germans, who had been sheltering in Dug-outs immediately came out and opened rapid fire with their machine guns. Some were seen to retire to the second and third lines. The enemy fought very well throwing Hand grenades into his own wire.

NOTES: A great many casualties were caused by the enemy's machine guns; infact the third and fourth waves suffered so heavily that by the time they had reached No Man's Land they had lost at least half their strength. Whole sections were wiped out.

The German front line wire was found to be almost intact, particularly on the left.

A few men of both "A" and "C" Coys managed to enter the German trenches on the right of the attack, but in all other parts of the line men were held up, being shot down by the Germans in front of them. The few survivors took shelter in shell holes in front of the German wire and remained there until they could get back under cover of darkness.

The failure of the attack was undoubtedly due to the wire not being sufficiently cut. Had this been cut the enemy's machine guns could have been dealt with by the men who managed to reach the front line. As it was, they could not be reached and there was no means of stopping their fire. Bombers attempted to silence them with grenades but could not reach them —consequently the succeeding waves were wiped out and did not arrive at the German wire in any strength.

- - - - - - -

FURTHER READING

There is an enormous amount of literature on the 1916 Battle of the Somme, and most especially on the 'First Day', that few hours that seems to have mesmerised the British. The result is that there is very little indeed on the later battles of the Somme, that great struggle that heaved and ground its way through over one hundred and forty days of battle.

As an excellent guide to the intricacies of the Somme, I would suggest General Sir A H Farrar-Hockley's *The Somme*. Although almost twenty-five years old, it provides the best, small volume, comprehensive description of the 1916 battle. Lyn MacDonald's *Somme* is based largely on the recollections and writings of men who were there. It is well illustrated and has some good maps, and reads easily. The deservedly best known book on the first day of the battle is Martin Middlebrook's *First Day of the Somme*. It is based on testimony of numerous veterans and was first published in 1971; I do not think it has been out of print since. He is one of the few authors to handle the 1918 German offensive, in his 'The Kaiser's Battle'.

In recent years the Pals battalions of 31st Divsion have been very well served. The first of these books was the *Barnsley Pals* (Jon Cooksey), followed swiftly by the *Accrington Pals* (Bill Turner), the *Sheffield City Battalion* (Ralph Gibson and Paul Oldfield) and the *Leeds Pals* (Laurie Milner) – all of these are available from Pen and Sword Books. They are printed in large format, have considerable detail on the establishment and training of ther battalion involved and are lavishly illustrated. They all have medal rolls, and some have casualty lists, places of burial, original lists of the men who enlisted and so forth. They are excellent value for money and at the time of writing are all in print.

92 (Hull Pals) Brigade has a history of its own, on a far less grand scale than the above; *This Righteous War* by B S Barnes. This book covers the whole war.

John Harris's, *The Covenant with Death* is a novel based upon the story of the Sheffield City Battalion. It is excellent.

There are numerous guides to the Somme Battlefield. Rose Coombs' *Before Endeavours Fade* is a good general introduction. This has been joined by two guides specifically for the Somme. Major and Mrs Holt's *Battlefield Guide to the Somme* is a sumptuously produced colour guide of some 250 pages, accompanied by a most useful separate map, which indicates all the cemeteries, memorials, places of interest and so forth. Martin and Mary Middlebrook have produced *The Somme Battlefields*, which covers British military interest from Crecy to the end of the Second World War. It is based on extensive knowledge of the battlefield, and besides being an excellent guide, is also a good read. Gerald Gliddon's *When the Barrage Lifts* is a village by village, wood by wood account of the battle, based on a vast knowledge of the literature on the war.

SELECTIVE INDEX